Unexpected Findings

50+ CLEVER JEWELRY DESIGNS **featuring everyday components**

Michelle Mach

INTERWEAVE.
interweave.com

D0128972

Editor ▪ Michelle Bredeson

Technical Editor ▪ Jane Dickerson

Associate Art Director ▪ Julia Boyles

Design ▪ Brenda Gallagher

Illustrator ▪ Ann Swanson

Photographer ▪ Joe Coca

Photo Stylist ▪ Ann Swanson

Production ▪ Katherine Jackson

Interweave
A division of F+W Media, Inc.
4868 Innovation Drive
Fort Collins, CO 80525
interweave.com

Manufactured in China by RR Donnelley
Shenzhen.

Library of Congress Cataloging-
in-Publication Data

Mach, Michelle.
Unexpected findings : 50+ clever jewelry
designs featuring everyday
components / Michelle Mach.
pages cm
Includes index.
ISBN 978-1-62033-600-7 (pbk.)
ISBN 978-1-62033-602-1 (PDF)
1. Jewelry making. 2. Jewelry settings.
3. Found objects (Art) I. Title.
TT212.M2635 2014
745.594'2--dc23

2014005778

10 9 8 7 6 5 4 3 2 1

Dedication

To Neal Krawetz, for encouraging me to follow my dreams

Acknowledgments

There may be only one name on the cover, but this book was a Herculean team effort. I'd like to express my deepest thanks to:

Editorial Director Allison Korleski, who championed the idea of this book from its infancy.

My editor, Michelle Bredeson, who provided a steady, smart, and calming influence during the typical ups-and-downs of a first-time author. I learned more from you than you realize.

Jane Dickerson, Cassie Armstrong, and Erica Smith for eagle-eyed editing; Brenda Gallagher for a stunning design; Joe Coca, Ann Swanson, and Julia Boyles for spectacular photos and styling (especially with those pesky jump rings!); Hollie Hill, for cheerfully and promptly answering my many administrative emails; Kate Wilson at *Beadwork* magazine for answering my questions about seed beads; Nancy Arndt for excellent proof-reading; and Kerry Bogert, for her insight during the project selection process.

My all-star design team: Lorelei Eurto, Jamie Hogsett, Denise Yezbak Moore, Erin Prais-Hintz, Molly Schaller, Erin Siegel, Erin Strother, Barb Switzer, Andrew Thornton, and Cindy Wimmer. I appreciate your hard work, creativity, and flexibility. I'd work with each of you again in a heartbeat.

My mom, for proudly wearing my earliest handmade jewelry; my dad and brother, both authors themselves, for showing me how it's done; and my friend Jan who accompanied me to early jewelry-making classes. Who knew where a little wire wrapping could lead?

And last but far from least, the many jewelry makers, bead artists, and shop owners I've met in person and online over the years: you inspire me every day.

Contents

THE PROJECTS

108

110

94

WISH

90

98

Introduction

Beads are the stars on the jewelry stage. They're the ones twirling, singing, and shouting while the findings scuttle backstage, working the lights and opening and closing the red velvet curtains. Ever wonder what would happen if their roles were reversed?

One of my earliest magazine submissions shone a spotlight on that very question. I'd created an agate-and-pearl necklace that seemed *almost* right. With the deadline coming up quickly, I didn't have the luxury of shopping for the perfect finishing touch. Rummaging through some drawers, I found a package of copper cones, the kind normally used to corral the ends of multistrand necklaces. I added them to chain as empty dangles and sold the design to *Jewelry Stringing* magazine.

This habit of using findings for something other than their intended purpose became a hallmark of my work. Not only was it fun to turn ring shanks into earrings or empty knot cups into darling dangles, but it led to an unexpected benefit as well.

I love buying findings, in part because I've convinced myself it's practical. It may take me years to figure out how to use those orange-and-magenta striped ceramic tubes, but I could use that silver toggle over the weekend. Did you notice that important word? *Could.* Yes, I'm talking about stash guilt. All those findings you already own that you *could* use, but aren't. You know what I mean: there are those hundred gunmetal spacer bars in the completely wrong size and those fold-over bails you bought before you learned you prefer wire-wrapped bails. If you stick exclusively with the by-the-book rules for using findings, we may all be living in a colony on Mars before you see the bottom of your findings drawer.

It doesn't need to be that way. All those findings can be used, just maybe not in the way you originally intended. I've gathered fifty all-new necklace, bracelet, and earring projects that use common findings such as jump rings, head pins, and clasps in unusual ways. (These "featured findings" are set in colored type in the materials list of each project to make them easy to find.) Along with my designs, you'll see creative jewelry projects from all-star designers Lorelei Eurto, Jamie Hogsett, Denise Yezbak Moore, Erin Prais-Hintz, Molly Schaller, Erin Siegel, Erin Strother, Barb Switzer, Andrew Thornton, and Cindy Wimmer.

Whether you make one project or dozens, I hope you'll be inspired to use findings in your own unique ways. Now pick a finding, any finding, and repeat after me: *What if . . . ?*

—Michelle

Make It Your Own

Years ago I visited a bead shop with a friend. She loved a pretty fuchsia-and-green glass necklace on display, but the exact beads were no longer available. She didn't feel confident about making substitutions and left empty-handed.

Sound familiar? It can be frustrating to learn that beads and findings come and go. Just as you might have trouble finding a swimsuit in December or bell bottoms after the 1960s have passed, that exact bead or chain or clasp might no longer be manufactured. What can you do?

While it might feel scary at first, deviating from a published design will help you discover your own artistic voice. Start small. Substitute an 8mm navy round for an 8mm green round. Changing just one aspect, such as color, and keeping others, such as size and shape the same, minimizes the risk that you'll be unhappy with the final result. As you gain experience, you'll be able to zero in not only on the materials used in a design, but also on the structure, mood, and techniques, and you'll be able to customize it even further.

Once you start making changes to a design, it's possible to move so far away from the original design that you'll have created something completely different. Still having doubts? Take a look at the variations that the designers and I created for many of the projects. With a little practice, you, too, can learn to use findings your way.

Findings

A definition for findings can be . . . surprisingly hard to find!
Everyone agrees that you need these small components to create finished jewelry, but jewelry makers differ on what precisely falls into this category. Some include anything that isn't a bead, including pendants, spacers, or flexible beading wire, while others remove stringing and beadlike materials. Not only that, different people may use different names for the identical finding. In this section, you'll find descriptions of the most common findings, along with common alternative names and a few simple design ideas.

BAILS

A bail is used to connect a pendant to the center of a necklace. Here are the most common kinds:

briolette bails ①
These bails have two pointed ends that you push together to close. As the name suggests, they're often used with briolettes, or teardrop-shaped beads.
Also called: pinch bails, ice-pick bails, prong bails

donut bails ②
These specialized bails work with donuts, those oversized round discs with a large hole in the middle. Slide the bail over the top of the donut and pinch closed.
Also called: donut holders

foldover bails ③
Two different bails claim this name. One looks like a long, flat metal strip with decorative ends. Dab glue on the ends and fold around your pendant, leaving an open loop at the top that you can use to string the pendant. The other foldover bail looks like a disc that has been folded in half. The folded part goes on your stringing material, while the attached jump ring fastens to your pendant.

The foldover bails used in these earrings look like tiny purses when paired with links from penny chain.

glue-on bails ⑦
These popular bails work with objects that don't have holes, such as Scrabble tiles, dominoes, or glass squares. Dab glue on the flat textured pad and press it against the item. Widely available Aanraku bails feature a distinctive leaf shape. Glue-ins are slightly different in that they have a center spike below the bail that you glue inside a hole. They're often used for large-holed beads. Let the glue dry thoroughly before hanging.
Also called: Aanraku bails, glue-on flat pads, glue-on foldovers, glue-ins, bead caps with loop glue-ins, cabochon bails

BAILS

hidden-loop bails ④

These bails have a loop at the back of the bail to hang your pendant.

hinged bails ⑤

These make a great choice if you want your pendants to be interchangeable. Open and close the bail whenever you want to change the look of the necklace.

loop bails ⑥

A similar idea to the second type of foldover bail, this bail features a larger, triangular-shaped opening that slides over your stringing material. You'll need a jump or split ring to attach your pendant to the loop.
Also called: bails with drop

rivet bails ⑧

These bails include a hole between the front and back for a rivet (such as a tiny nail) that will secure them to a metal pendant.

screw pegs ⑨

Insert these components into half-drilled items, gluing to secure. If you make your own polymer clay pendants, you can insert these into soft clay and bake to set.
Also called: top pins

snap-on bails ⑩

To use, open the folded tab, slide on the pendant, and close. You may wish to glue the folded tab shut since it can pop open easily.
Also called: spring bail

BEAD CAPS AND CONES

BEAD CAPS AND CONES

Bead caps cover the tops and bottoms of beads, adding texture and color to an otherwise plain beaded strand. Cones attractively hide the ends of multistrand necklaces and bracelets. Many bead caps and cones look like other objects (trees, spider webs, sea urchins, or ice cream cones), making it easy to come up with unusual uses.

bead caps ①

Use bead caps on either side of a bead to provide extra texture. A double-sided bead cap makes for a sleeker design, replacing two bead caps with one.

cones ②

Hide the messy ends of a multistrand necklace under a cone.

Acorn-patterned bead caps and brown ceramic rounds make an easy fall necklace.

This copper-plated cone looks irresistibly like the edible kind, especially when paired with a ceramic round the color of Neapolitan ice cream.

BEZELS AND BEAD FRAMES

Both bezels and bead frames add a decorative border around beads or pendants. See "No Hole? No Problem!" (page 17) for more ideas on how to use bezels and bezel tape.

bezels ①

Use a bezel to frame a cabochon or rhinestones or to create a mixed-media pendant. You'll need glue to attach the cabochon, unless the bezel contains enough prongs along its edges to hold the cabochon securely in place.

Also called: cameo mounts, settings

bezel tape

This finding looks like a long strip of lacy metal that can be cut into different lengths and wound around a cabochon. Despite its name, it's not a sticky product with adhesive.

Also called: bezel lace, ribbon bezel, lace-edge bezel, setting bezel

bead frames ②

These metal squares, rectangles, and circles might look like links/connectors (see page 12) because of the empty space in the middle. However, they also have vertical holes at the top and bottom. To give the illusion that a bead is floating with the frame, string the bottom hole of the frame on an eye or head pin, add a bead, string the top hole of the frame, and form a loop.

BRACELET AND RING FINDINGS

Bracelet and ring findings offer blank canvases for creating quick jewelry with glue, wire, and simple embellishments.

bracelet bases ①

Typically made of metal, these solid bracelets come in a number of styles such as bangles, cuffs, or cha-cha bracelets. A round bangle forms a complete circle. It can be plain, channeled, or studded with loops. Wider than a bangle, a cuff forms a C shape. It can have predrilled holes for rivets or a bezel setting. A cha-cha bracelet has a stretchy base with allover loops for dangles. Leather bracelet cuffs with attached snaps or other closures are an increasingly popular option.

ring bases ②

Sold flat or already curved into a round shape, ring bases may be precisely sized or adjustable with an open gap at the back. Some have attached bezels or loops just like their bracelet counterparts. Others look like flat pieces of filigree that you can bend around a mandrel or ring sizer to get the proper shape.

Also called: ring bands, ring shanks

BEZELS AND BEAD FRAMES

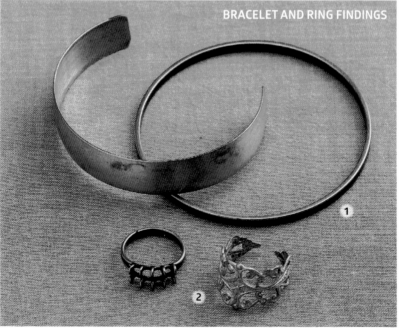

BRACELET AND RING FINDINGS

CLASPS

Clasps provide closure for your bracelets and necklaces.

ball-chain connectors ①
To use these inexpensive clasps, snap one ball of ball chain into each end of the clasp.

barrel clasps ②
The ends of this clasp screw together to secure. Named for its shape, it widens in the middle and has two raised lines on either side that look like the metal bars around a wooden barrel.

box clasps ③
These highly decorative clasps often feature gemstones, carved shells, or found objects such as coins. To close, insert the folded tab of metal into the open slot on the box. Over time, the tab may wear out. Occasionally, you'll see box clasps with a safety chain.

buckles ④
With the popularity of leather bracelets, these are becoming more common. They work by inserting the leather end through the metal bars as you might use a belt.

foldover clasps ⑤
Not to be confused with a foldover cord end, this rectangular hinged clasp folds open and snaps shut to close.
Also called: bracelet foldover clasps

hook-and-eye clasps ⑥
A simple clasp, the hook-and-eye blends seamlessly into most wire or chain designs. Since these fasteners work by tension, use them at the back of necklaces with beads heavy enough to keep the clasp closed. (Lightweight pearls, Lucite, or tiny beads of any kind won't weigh enough to secure the clasp.) The eye half of the clasp may look like a figure eight. If you find hooks alone, you can pair them with a soldered jump ring.

lobster clasps ⑦
Commonly used with chain, a lobster clasp opens with a lever on the side and hooks to a metal tag, a jump ring, or split ring. It's a popular choice for designers who sell jewelry because the clasp can be hooked to any link in the chain, giving the buyer some sizing flexibility. Small lobster clasps can be difficult for people with mobility issues to open. The swivel clasp is a variation that turns at its base, making it easier to open and close.
Also called: lobster claws, swivel clasps, trigger clasps

magnetic clasps ⑧
Magnetic clasps work well for those with mobility issues. Some designers prefer to use them only in necklaces, since the strong magnets easily attach themselves to metal folding chairs or other surfaces near your wrist. People with pacemakers should not use them, as the magnets can interfere with the device.

CLASPS

Multistrand Clasps

These clasps use multiple loops to accommodate several strands. Use them when you want to keep each strand separate and evenly spaced. Box, hook-and-eye, magnetic, slide-lock, and toggle clasps all come in multistrand forms. While two- and three-loop multistrand clasps are common, it's possible to find ones with a dozen loops.

pearl clasps ⑨

Decorated with filigree and shaped like an eye, these clasps appear mostly on traditional pearl necklaces. They have a folding hook that slides in and out at an angle and then snaps into place.
Also called: fishhook clasps, filigree clasps

S-clasps ⑩

Shaped like an elongated version of the letter, an S-clasp often closes with a jump ring. Like the hook-and-eye, it makes an unobtrusive clasp ideal for necklaces or bangle-style bracelets.

slide-lock clasps ⑪

This tube-shaped clasp, usually multistrand with two to five loops, slides apart to open. It twists and clicks into place to close. Some versions may also be magnetic.
Also called: tube bars, tube slides

snap clasps ⑫

To close this clasp, press the rounded, doorknob-shaped end into the open circle. Snap clasps are best used for lightweight pieces, since too much weight (such as a strand of heavy gemstones) will cause the clasp to pop open.
Also called: trailer hitches, ball-and-sockets

spring-ring clasps ⑬

These work similarly to lobster clasps and have a little lever on the side that opens and closes. Their round shape can blend more easily into designs than a lobster clasp. They're best for lightweight designs, since the thin loop connecting the clasp to the necklace or bracelet can break easily.
Also called: spring-rings, bolt rings

toggle clasps ⑭

Widely available toggle clasps have two parts: a ring and a bar. The ring does not have to be a circle; it can be a star, heart, or other shape. Toggle clasps need tension to work; the heaviness of the beads causes the bar to pull tight against the ring. With lightweight pieces, such as a simple pearl bracelet, the toggle will come undone. You'll find a huge range of toggles, including many artisan-made ones that may be featured at the front or side of a necklace.
Also called: bar-and-ring toggles

CORD & RIBBON FINDINGS

These findings neatly finish ribbon and cord ends and provide a loop for connecting a clasp.

crimp cord ends ①

These work well for rounded leather cords. Insert the cord into the finding and use your flat-nose pliers to flatten the crimp end. Depending upon the design, some may be flattened in the middle and others near the tips of the cord end. Some may also include an attached hook at the top that can be paired with a crimp cord end with a loop. Glue may be used if desired.
Also called: crimp end caps

end coils ②

These look like tiny springs with a loop at the end. Dab glue inside the finding and insert your round cord.
Also called: cord coils

foldover cord ends ③

To use these, slide the end of your flat cord or ribbon inside the finding. Fold the left and right sides of the cord end closed using your flat-nose pliers. If desired, add a dab of glue before closing.

CORD & RIBBON FINDINGS

knot cups ④

Place the knot at the end of your strung piece inside the open hole at the bottom of a knot cup and close with crimping pliers. The loop on the opposite end will attach to your clasp or jump ring. Sometimes you'll see knot cups that are patterned to look like a shell.
Also called: bead tips, clamshells, clam shells, calottes

ribbon ends ⑤

These findings look like a book with a loop in the middle of the tiny spine. They're often, but not always, patterned with a basketweave pattern. Once you slide in your ribbon and close the end, the teeth on the edges will grip the material. You may also wish to use a dab of glue before closing.
Also called: basketweave crimps, ribbon clamps

These metal knot cups add a musical quality to these dangle earrings, as they jangle against the beads. I've added a tiny size 15° seed bead inside the knot cup for extra musicality.

Ducking for Cover

HIDING CRIMPS

If you don't want to use crimp covers, here are some other ways to hide your crimps:

USE JUMP RINGS: You can either simply string them on (see Key West, page 104) or make chain maille rosettes (see Rings Around the Monarch, page 66).

USE BEADED CAMOUFLAGE: Use tiny spacers the same color as the crimps before and/or after them. The crimps will still be in plain sight, but they'll be hard to identify. I especially like corner-less cubes for this purpose.

USE DANGLES: On bracelets, make multiple wire-wrapped dangles and charms and string them over the crimped end.

USE RIBBON: Knot a short piece of pretty ribbon over the crimps. Wide, frayed ribbon, such as sari ribbon, works especially well.

USE CONES: Yes, even if it isn't a multistrand piece, you can still use cones to cover up crimped ends.

CRIMPS

Essential for long-lasting jewelry, crimps secure the flexible beading wire to the clasp of a necklace or bracelet.

crimp tubes ① and beads ②

Both crimp tubes and crimp beads perform the same function: holding the clasp to the end of the flexible beading wire. However, the tools to use them differ. The tubes require crimping pliers, while the beads need flat-nose pliers. Twisted crimps look pretty when flattened. Crimp end caps, not to be confused with the finding of the same name used with cords, include a loop above the crimp tube.

crimp covers ③

These C-shaped pieces of metal fit over your crimped tubes. They are available in different sizes; use one size larger than your crimp size. (For example, for a 2mm crimp tube, use a 3mm cover.) Hold the crimp cover over the crimped tube and use your crimping pliers to close. (Some beaders prefer using chain-nose pliers.) It will look like a round bead when closed. For the prettiest results, make sure the seam of the crimp cover will be at the back of your piece.

wire guards ④

Wire guards slide over the ends of flexible beading wire and protect that vulnerable stretch between the end of the crimp and the clasp.
Also called: wire guardians, wire protectors, cable thimbles

EARRING FINDINGS

Ranging from small to large and plain to ornate, these findings keep earrings attached to the ear.

chandeliers ①

These elaborate findings contain multiple loops at the bottom to attach dangles and are paired with other earring findings to attach to the ear. They're often filigree and are round or teardrop shaped.

clip-ons ②

These earrings for nonpierced ears have a loop to attach dangles. They either open and close with a hinge, or they have a screw that tightens and loosens the earring.
Also called: earscrews, earclips

ear threads ③

These look like very fine, long pieces of chain and go through the earlobe.
Also called: earring strings

hooks ④

The most common type of ear wire, they are usually rounded in shape

CRIMPS

with a loop for attaching dangles and are often decorated above the loop with a coil of wire or a single bead. *Also called: French hooks, fish hooks, shepherd's crook ear wires*

hoops ⑤
A continuous circle of wire with a little hole at the end, hoops range dramatically in size with some as large as bangle bracelets.
Also called: beading hoops

kidney wires ⑥
Kidney wires feature a large kidney-shaped wire with a small loop near the bottom for adding lightweight dangles. The hook wire closure makes them less likely to accidentally fall off.
Also called: safety ear wires

leverbacks ⑦
These findings offer extra security for the wearer, since the back of the earring folds up against the ear.
Also called: lever backs, hinged ear wires

posts ⑧
The short, stiff wire on post earrings goes through the ear. It's closed with an ear nut, sometimes called a butterfly back.
Also called: studs, bullets

FILIGREE
Filigree is a lacy piece of metal finding with numerous decorative holes. Filigree components may be used as simple pendants or charms, which fall into the materials category, but they also serve as connectors, findings that link items together. Filigree components bend easily, so with a little work you can also create tube beads or create findings such as bails, ribbon cord ends, bezels, or hook clasps. Findings such as bead caps, chandelier earring components, cones, and clasps may be made with filigree. Whichever category they belong to, you'll find they're indispensable for creating jewelry.

HEAD AND EYE PINS
Head pins and eye pins are short, straight wires that can be bent to create dangles or links.

head pins ①
Use these wires with a flat end for creating beaded dangles. Decorative head pins can feature flowers, beads, or other interesting elements. You may occasionally see double-headed head pins ③ that can be wrapped around elements as an embellishment.

eye pins ②
Use these wires with a simple loop at one end to create beaded links.

FILIGREE

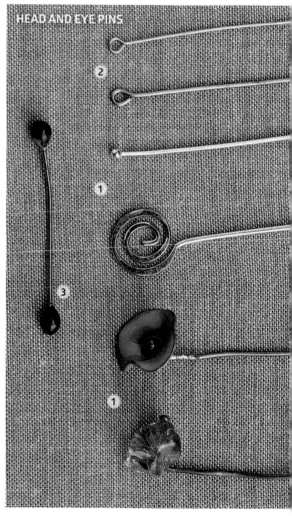
HEAD AND EYE PINS

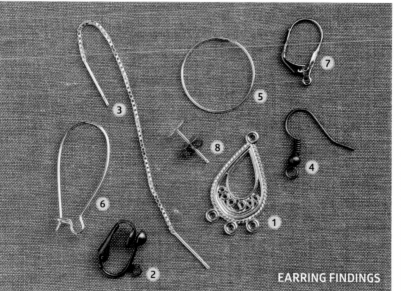
EARRING FINDINGS

JUMP RINGS AND SPLIT RINGS

Use jump rings and split rings to connect elements such as clasps, chain, beaded links, charms, and pendants.

jump rings ①

These round, oval, square, and rectangular wires connect elements together. They're sold unsoldered, or open, making it possible for you to open and close them as needed. Soldered or closed jump rings make more secure connections for a closure that gets a lot of wear and tear. You can find locking jump rings ②, which, as their name suggests, pop together for a more secure connection, but they cost considerably more.

split rings ③

Unlike jump rings, which have a little gap between the ends of the circular wire, the ends of split rings pass each other, making the rings a little more secure. They're good to use for charms or dangles or as connectors on clasps. If you own a key chain, it likely uses a very large, heavy-duty split ring.

LINKS/CONNECTORS

A huge, diverse category, links, or connectors, have one or more holes, usually at the ends, although some have holes on every side or a single one in the middle. If a connector has an uneven number of holes, it usually has a label, such as 2-to-1 or 3-to-1 connector. Connectors make quick earrings, and linking several together can create a necklace focal point. You might also sometimes hear about "fastenables," which are normally sold as items that can be riveted, or bracelet bars, which have a hole on either end and a slightly curved appearance. Both of these generally also fall into this category. Washer Woman (page 62) uses hardware-store washers as connectors.
Also called: end bar links

JUMP RINGS AND SPLIT RINGS

LINKS/CONNECTORS

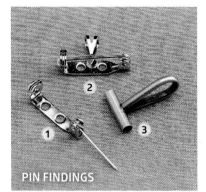

PIN FINDINGS

Pin findings allow you to easily create pins or brooches or turn them into pendants.

pin backs ①

Glue one of these findings to the back of an item to turn it into a pin. One of my favorite variations is the bail pin back ②, which as the name suggests, has a bail attached to the top. This makes it possible for you to design a pendant that can also be worn as a pin. How cool is that?
Also called: brooch backs, brooch bars

pin converters ③

Whenever I hear about someone hacking up a valuable vintage brooch to repurpose it, I cringe. If you want to wear an old brooch as a pendant, there's an easy solution: a pin converter. Slide the tube on the pin converter over the pin on your brooch. Use the attached loop at the top to string the brooch-turned-pendant onto a necklace.
Also called: brooch converters

SPACER BARS

Designed to keep multiple strands of strung beads in orderly lines, spacer bars typically have between two and five holes, but can have more.
Also called: separator bars, bead bars, aligners, strandage bars, bracelet bars

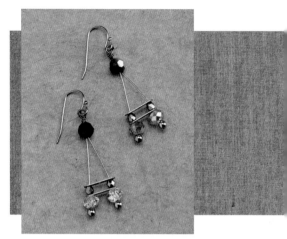

Spacer bars come in all sizes, even ones small enough for earrings.

SPECIALIZED FINDINGS

At any bead shop or show, you'll see many more findings than the typical ones discussed here. Some less common findings include bead cages ① (an oval-shaped wire cage that fits over one or more beads), necklace extenders ② (large, rounded rectangular clasps), bola tips (for bolo ties), foldover chain connectors (to use instead of jump rings to make chain), and perforated discs used for cagework. Numerous findings exist for a single material or use, often created by a single manufacturer. For example, there's a special bail designed to work only with a key-shaped Swarovski crystal. There's also a double-loop clasp that's meant for lariat-style necklaces ③. If you can imagine it, chances are it exists!

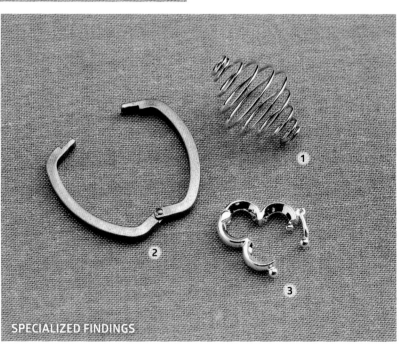

From Plain to Pretty:

HOW TO JAZZ UP ORDINARY FINDINGS

Just because you buy a plain finding doesn't mean you are stuck using it as is. Any mixed-media technique, from rubber stamping to resin, can add a unique touch to a finding. Try these low-tech options that don't require specialized metalsmithing materials, such as a torch or jeweler's saw:

ADDING PATINA ①

Use a hard-boiled egg, liver of sulfur, or a commercial blackening agent to darken bright metals such as sterling silver and copper. For brass or copper, a mix of salt and vinegar potato chips, plus extra white vinegar, produces pretty greens overnight. After darkening your metals, you can use a polishing cloth or fine steel wool to highlight the raised areas on your metal. *Rustic Wrappings* by Kerry Bogert (Interweave, 2012) contains several patina recipes. No matter which recipe you try, use a clean metal item without any sealants for best results.

FORMING

Just because a finding arrives flat or curved doesn't mean it needs to stay that way. Using your hands or pliers (flat-nose or bail-making, depending upon your goal), you can unbend rings or bead caps to use as flat connectors or bend pieces of filigree into clasps and bails. Curve a long piece of metal to make a comfortable bracelet connector or simply to add a little flare to an ordinary design.

BREAKING OR CUTTING ②

It's easy to accidentally break thin filigree, so why not do it on purpose? Bend filigree back and forth until it breaks to create smaller shapes from a large piece. Wear thin work gloves to protect your hands from cuts and use your flat-nose pliers to bend the piece. File the sharp edges of the filigree before using it in your jewelry. Alternatively, you may be able to cut metal with shears from the hardware store.

EMBELLISHING WITH WIRE, RIBBON, BEADS, AND MORE ③

Simple wire wrapping with or without beads can add beauty to a simple clasp or other finding and make your component an integral part of your design. Ribbon or cord adds a touch of softness. Finish with a knot or use a combination of ribbon and beads.

HAMMERING AND METAL STAMPING ④

Hammer your metal for texture using the round end of an ordinary ball-peen hammer or a specialized texturing hammer. Metal stamping allows you to add messages and symbols to your design. It's amazing how just changing a surface from smooth to bumpy gives the piece a completely different feel.

HOLE PUNCHING

If the material is thin enough, you can use a metal hole punch to add holes, turning a charm into a two-hole connector or a chandelier drop. You can add holes for functional reasons, such as wrapping two solid pieces together or turning a solid object into a charm. Holes can also be added purely for decoration, turning a plain bead cap into a whimsical polka-dot creation.

MIXING AND MATCHING

Just because you buy a toggle clasp does not mean you're obligated to use the ring and bar together. Mix up parts from different sets or create your own. Anything with a ring, such as a washer or a round connector, could be a toggle ring; a bar could be created with a heavy-gauge eye pin or a piece of wire that is strong enough to bear the weight of the jewelry. Lobster clasps normally close with a jump ring, but anything with a large-enough hole (a piece of filigree, a chandelier finding, a connector) will work, too. Make your own loop bail by combining a wrapped loop with a filigree tube.

PAINTING ⑤

Gilder's Paste adds a metallic sheen, while solid colorants, such as Swellegant or Vintaj patinas, add blocks of color. Alcohol inks run together, creating a tie-dye or watercolor effect. Model paint also works well. You will need to seal the paint with a clear coat of Permalac, Krylon, or other clear sealant. You may need to use a paintbrush for sealing; spray paints can cause some colorants, such as alcohol inks, to run.

Other Materials

Findings are like chocolate: delicious, but not suitable alone for a complete, healthy diet. To create a satisfying design, you'll want a full serving of beads, pendants, charms, stringing materials, and other items.

BEADS

From mass-produced beads at your local craft store to one-of-a-kind handmade treasures from your favorite bead artist, beads add color, texture, and life to your jewelry. They help convey mood and theme and may even serve as the inspiration for the entire design. Popular materials for beads include ceramic, crystal, gemstones, glass, metal, polymer clay, bone, shell, and wood. They come in all sorts of shapes: rounds, squares, coins, rondelles, discs, teardrops, bicones, chips, barrels, and tubes. They may be matte or shiny, smooth or textured. Sizes range from tiny size 15° seed beads to extra-large beads measuring 40mm or larger.

BUTTONS AND SEQUINS

Buttons (and their sequin cousins) are refugees from the sewing world. Not exactly beads or findings, they're often overlooked by jewelry designers. While you can simply string them on beading wire, here are a few other ideas:

links/connectors

Flat buttons with two or four holes make great links/connectors between chain or other elements. See Lotus Blossom necklace (page 30) as an example.

clasps

Buttons with shanks make beautiful custom clasps when paired with a loop made of cords or seed beads. See Leaves of Gold necklace (page 48) as an example.

dangles

Buttons with holes and top-holed sequins (properly called paillettes) make cute dangles. Thin sequins are easily bent, so use them for jewelry that won't get a lot of wear, such as earrings, or in pairs. See Gypsy Girl bracelet (page 50) as an example of doubled paillettes used as bracelet dangles.

spacers

Sequins with center holes make great thin spacers for times when you want a splash of color but are short on space. Since they're so lightweight, you can pair them with heavier beads to keep your jewelry comfortably wearable.

Don't have time for a trip to the fabric store? You can make your own custom buttons by adding holes to almost any object.

CABOCHONS

Commonly called "cabs," cabochons are typically round or oval with a curved front side and flat back. They may be made from gemstones, glass, resin, or other materials. Their lack of holes can present a challenge to designers.

CHARMS

Typically made from metal, charms feature a top loop for hanging from a jump ring. They often represent specific subjects, such as flowers, sports, or animals, making them especially popular for simple earrings and charm bracelets.

If you love beading, your stash will quickly grow to include hundreds of beads, charms, pendants, buttons, sequins, cabochons, and spacers.

No Hole? No Problem!

HOW TO TURN A CABOCHON INTO A PENDANT

Beadweavers create elaborate frames for cabochons using peyote stitch, netting, or other seed bead techniques, while advanced wire-workers may create ornate wire-wrapped cages. While those options produce stunning results, using cabochons in your designs doesn't have to require hours of work. Here are four quick-and-easy methods:

GLUE INTO A BEZEL

Choose a pretty bezel and glue your cabochon inside using a strong adhesive such as E-6000. (You may need to first roughen the surfaces to help them adhere.) This option works best for cabochons in standard sizes and shapes.

ADD A COMMERCIAL BAIL

If you have an unusually shaped cabochon, choose a glue-on bail. Add glue to the flat pad on the bail and adhere it to the back of the cabochon. You may want to first mark the spot where you'll glue the bail to ensure that you attach it straight and centered. This method works well for smaller, lightweight cabochons.

WRAP INSIDE A LARGE FILIGREE COMPONENT

A thin filigree component, easily bent, makes a very decorative case for a cabochon. Place your stone in the center of the large filigree component and bend the sides up to form a frame around the cabochon, keeping in mind where you'd like to place a jump ring or wire-wrapped loop for hanging. Use your hands or pliers to shape the filigree component.

WRAP WITH BEZEL TAPE

Cut a length that will encircle your cabochon with a little extra to create a small loop for a jump ring or wire-wrapped loop. Bend the prongs on one edge down and wrap it around the bottom of the cabochon. Wrap the top curves snugly around the cabochon's top, making sure that you've left two even lengths for the top. Fold the top part of the tape to create a loop and attach a wire-wrapped loop or jump ring. This method takes the most practice of the four, but the results can be very pretty.

From left to right: wrapping with filigree, using bezel tape, and gluing into a bezel.

PENDANTS

Pendants serve as the focal point for necklaces and are made of the same varied materials as beads. Their holes may run horizontally or vertically. Alternatively, they may have an attached bail loop for easy hanging. Some ways to hang pendants include commercially made bails, jump rings, and split rings, or by creating briolette wrapped loops, double-wrapped loop bails (see Rings Around the Monarch necklace, page 66), wrapped or simple loops, and lark's head knots (see Zero Hour necklace, page 70).

SPACERS

These thin, typically round, small discs add sparkle and interest when interspersed between beads in a plain beaded strand. While most items labeled for sale as spacers are metal, any small, thin bead made from any material can be used as a spacer. The daisy spacer, the most popular shape, looks like a flower when viewed head on.

STRINGING MATERIALS

While it's fun to admire pretty beads in a drawer, you'll need some kind of stringing material if you want to easily share their beauty with others.

flexible beading wire

Coated, flexible steel beading wire for stringing necklaces and bracelets comes in different thicknesses. Thinner wires (.014–.015) work best for lightweight materials with small holes such as pearls. Use medium wire (.018–.019) as an all-purpose wire for most projects, reserving the largest wire (.024) for heavy glass or gemstone beads. Beading wire also differs in flexibility, with 49-strand wire being the most flexible and least likely to kink. Normally covered with beads, exposed flexible beading wire in a bright color can add an unexpected twist to designs. Use several strands as tassels, weave it through chain, braid it for cuff-style bracelets, or connect small circles of it for chain.

braided and thermally bonded beading threads

Often used for beadweaving, these durable threads resist fraying. Braided beading thread, originally designed for the fishing industry, comes sized in terms of the pound test with 4 lb being thinner than 6 lb. It's available in limited colors: smoke, white, and green. Thermally bonded beading thread is stiffer, making it a good choice for pieces that need to hold their shape.

chain

Chain, usually a series of wire loops, comes in a variety of shapes and sizes. Popular types include ball, cable, curb, figaro, figure eight, ladder, oval, and rolo. Chain may be soldered or unsoldered. With soldered chain, the closed links must be cut apart and discarded if you need a shorter length. Unsoldered chain makes a more economical choice since you can open and close the chain links as you would jump rings. Heavy chain may require memory wire or hardware-store cutters to cut. Use chain for hanging pendants and for making charm bracelets, tassels, and looped fringe on chandelier earrings (see Midnight Waltz, page 64). You can also knot or braid thin chain (sometimes called stringing chain) as you would cord or ribbon (see Fringe Benefits variation, page 44).

Don't forget using chain links for chain! I know what you're thinking: isn't that like those homemade yogurt recipes that begin "Start with a cup of yogurt"? But specialty chain can be pricey. Combine fancy individual chain links with your own jump rings or connectors to stretch your beading budget.

cord and ribbon

Some popular types of cord and ribbon include douppioni silk ribbon, crepe cord, suede lace, linen cord, silk cord, and sari ribbon. Your choice depends upon the mood you want to convey: romantic, rustic, sweet, exotic, fun. For example, the romantic Tidal Treasures necklace (page 57) uses dupioni silk, while the more casual Westward Bound earrings (page 28) uses suede lace.

Cord may be used for hanging pendants or woven through chain for extra color. Large, flat leather or suede cords make sturdy bracelets. Short bits of ribbon make nice embellishments tied on pendants, used as tassels (A Passel of Tassels, page 100), or in between beads. They can also be used in lieu of a clasp. Keep in mind that ribbon does fray, although you can add fabric sealant to the ends to keep them smooth.

gauged wire

Use this wire for wrapping, making loops, coils, or spirals. The higher the gauge, the thinner the wire. Thin 26-gauge wire works best for decorative details such as wire wrapping. Generally, 20- to 22-gauge might be used to create dangles or ear wires. Thick, heavy-gauge wire (14 to 18) works well for clasps or bangle forms that need to hold their shape. Colorful craft wire, often a coated copper, should be tested to make sure that the color won't chip off as you work. Using nylon-jaw pliers will help minimize accidental scratching of the wire.

Your choice of ribbon, cord, chain, gauged wire, or flexible beading wire will not only impact the look and wearability of your jewelry design, but also its cost.

DIY Chain

Making your own chain helps your designs stand out. Here are a few things to consider when choosing elements for chain:

EXPENSE: Some findings are expensive, so mix them with less expensive items or use them for short pieces of chain.

WEIGHT: You'll want the chain to hang correctly and not twist around. Using two jump rings rather than a single one in between them helps weigh down lightweight elements.

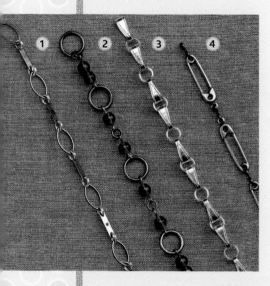

FLEXIBILITY: For a chain with a lot of movement, choose smaller elements.

FUNCTIONALITY: Using clasps to join your chain since this lets you take apart and reconfigure your chain in different ways.

Need ideas for components to combine? Try these.

FLEXIBLE BEADING WIRE: Whether plain or strung with beads, use loops of flexible beading wire closed with crimps for colorful links.

JUMP RINGS: These come in different sizes and shapes, such as triangles, rectangles, and flowers. While you can make chain entirely of open, unsoldered jump rings, you can also use them to connect other elements.

SPACER BARS: Be careful of using extra-long bars if you want to maintain a fluid, curved look. ①

EARRING FINDINGS: Chandelier findings make delicate chain.

EYE PINS: String eye pins with beads to make colorful links and connectors. ②

BAILS: Any type of bail that has an open connection at each end, such as a loop bail or foldover bail, can be used. ③

KNOT CUPS: Connect these with jump rings or use them as dangles for fancy chain.

LINKS/CONNECTORS OR FILIGREE COMPONENTS: These come in a huge range of sizes and designs, such as flowers, rings, and gears. Remember you can make your own links/connectors by punching holes in metal blanks, Scrabble tiles, or almost anything else you desire.

FOLDOVER CHAIN CONNECTORS: Use these folded pieces of metal instead of jump rings to connect elements. ④

CHARMS: Sometimes you can find charms that have extra holes in the design. ④

GLUES AND ADHESIVES

You may sometimes find it necessary to use glue in your jewelry. Two popular all-purpose choices include E-6000 and superglue. To find the right glue for your project, start by finding glues that work with your specific materials, such as paper, metal, fabric, or wood. Then look at toxicity, drying time, price, and ease of use. Use glue in well-ventilated areas as most produce toxic fumes. It helps to use a toothpick to dab the glue into small areas such as cord or ribbon ends. Sometimes you'll need to clamp the item while drying; the pressure will help the glue adhere. You also may find it necessary to first roughen smooth items with sandpaper before gluing for better adhesion. In any case, let any glued item dry thoroughly before proceeding to the next step of your project.

METAL BLANKS

Metal blanks come in sterling silver, copper, brass, bronze, aluminum, and plated base metals. The shapes, sizes, and gauges vary. As with gauged wire, the larger the number, the thinner and more pliable the metal blank. Blanks may or may not have predrilled holes. You may add holes yourself and turn a blank into a pendant, charm, or link/connector. While they're popularly used with metal stamping, metal blanks can be a great layered element when hammered (see Ancient Artifacts earrings, page 84).

Tools

You can make amazing jewelry with only a few tools. For years, my jewelry toolbox consisted of a few pairs of pliers and wire cutters. While you can make most of the projects in this book with just the basics, having a few extras, such as a metal hole-punch tool, will broaden your jewelry-making options considerably. While you'll probably want most of the tools in this section eventually, don't feel you need to buy them all at once or only in new, top-of-the-line condition. If you can, take a class where you'll be able to try different tools and see what you might like to own.

FORMING

These tools make loops, bends, curves, coils, and twists.

bail-making pliers ①

As their name suggests, these pliers with uniform cylindrical jaws turn wire or metal into pendant bails. Available in sizes from 2–21mm, you can also use them to form coils for jump rings or to bend filigree components for cuff bracelets and rings. You may be able to use the largest part of your round-nose pliers, a mandrel, or even your fingers as a substitute for bail-making pliers, depending upon the softness of the metal and what you need to do.

chain-nose pliers ②

Use these narrow-tipped, smooth pliers when wire wrapping, opening and closing jump rings, or finishing wrapped loops. Bent chain-nose pliers feature angled tips that make it even easier to reach tight places.

crimping pliers ③

These specialized pliers close the crimp tubes that attach the ends of flexible beading wire to clasps. You'll also find them handy for closing crimp covers and knot cups. While crimping pliers come in different sizes, the ones used with common 2–3mm crimps are probably the most useful. You can scoot by without this tool if you buy crimp beads (not tubes) and flatten them with your chain- or flat-nose pliers. See crimping in Basic Techniques (page 130) for instructions.

flat-nose pliers ④

You'll want two pairs of these (or one pair and a pair of chain-nose pliers) to open jump rings. The wide, smooth jaw allows you to firmly grasp the edges of jump rings or wire.

nylon-jaw pliers ⑤

These pliers do not leave marks on the wire, nor will they chip delicate crystal or glass beads. You can also use nylon-jaw pliers for straightening kinked wire. The nylon jaws can be replaced if they become too scratched. If you don't own nylon-jaw pliers, you can temporarily wrap the jaws of your pliers with painter's tape, which leaves less sticky residue than regular masking tape. Some beaders also like Tool Magic, a compound that temporarily affixes a rubber coating to the pliers.

ring-bending pliers

These pliers have an arched edge for transforming flat metal into curved ring bands. You might also be able to use them instead of bail-making pliers to bend filigree components.

round-nose pliers ⑥

With their rounded tips, these pliers help make perfectly

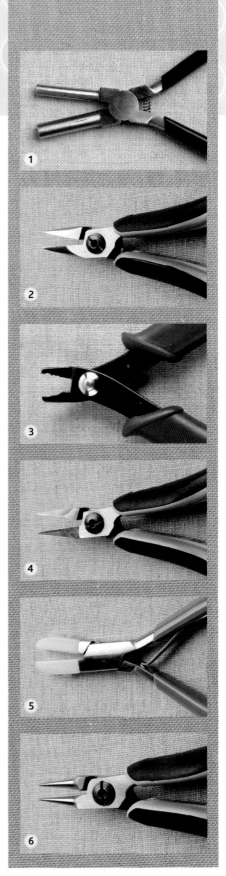

round simple and wrapped loops. Use a permanent marker on the barrels to mark the spot to make identically sized loops each time. If you can only splurge on one tool, this would be my choice. Be careful: some cheaper brands have not-quite-round barrels that will frustrate your attempts at round loops.

stepped pliers ⑦

With multiple barrels in graduated sizes, these pliers make me think of children on a staircase à la *The Sound of Music*. You may find these a more economical choice than buying multiple pairs of bail-making pliers in different sizes. A mandrel or round-nose pliers may make a workable substitute.

dowel or mandrel

Wood or steel bracelet and ring mandrels help you create consistently sized jewelry. If you're making coils for jump rings or decorative links, you can try a knitting needle, chopstick, marker, or any other object that is the size and shape you need.

CUTTING

These tools separate a large component into smaller pieces. While it's tempting to use the same scissors or cutters on all types of material, doing so will quickly ruin them. It may save you time, but it won't save you money!

scissors

You'll need several pairs to ensure that the blades don't dull too quickly. Fiskars children's scissors work best for cutting braided or thermally bonded beading thread. Use sharp sewing or embroidery scissors for cutting ribbon, cord, or fabric. Regular office scissors work fine for cutting paper. You can find heavy-duty metal shears or snips in the hardware store for cutting light gauges (typically 20–24) of metal.

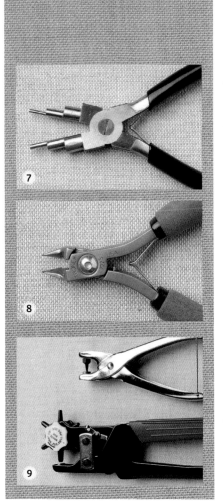

wire cutters ⑧

You'll want flush cutters to neatly cut gauged and flexible beading wire. Some designers prefer a separate pair for each, since different materials will cause different wear on the blades. For steel memory wire, use memory wire cutters; the stiff wire will destroy your good jewelry wire cutters. If you don't own memory wire cutters, use an inexpensive pair of wire cutters from the hardware store.

PUNCHING HOLES

These tools remove small circles from larger components.

hand drill

A hand drill from the hardware store gives you the most options in hole size and placement, as well as the widest range of drillable materials, including metal, wood, light plastic, and even paper. Be sure to use the appropriate type of drill bit for the material. A thick scrap of wood makes a good drilling surface, unless you want to turn your work surface into Swiss cheese. Remember to wear eye protection when working with the drill or your cutters.

leather hole punches ⑨

You'll find several kinds available at craft and hardware stores, including a rotary option that offers multiple hole sizes. Make sure that there's enough space between the jaws to insert two pieces of leather (or one folded piece). This will allow you to make evenly spaced holes for earrings or for attaching a clasp to bracelet. See page 130 in Basic Techniques for instructions.

metal hole-punch pliers

These work like a paper hole punch: insert the metal blank between the jaws and squeeze shut. The pliers come with replaceable tips, as they will eventually wear out or break. Because of the short jaws, these pliers work best for holes added near the edge of a component. Use them with soft metals (generally up to 18- to 20-gauge) with hole-size options of 1.25–1.8mm.

paper hole punch

Use a basic version from an office store or a fancy one from the scrapbooking section of the craft store. The fancier ones allow you to punch different-size holes as well as simple shapes. Some extra-sharp paper hole punches will work on light plastic (such as sequins) or soft leather.

permanent marker

It's helpful to mark the places to drill with a permanent marker. Remove the marks with a cotton ball dipped in rubbing alcohol. (Test it first, since rubbing alcohol might react with the finish of coated metal.)

screw-down metal hole punch

This tool offers two different-size holes (1.6 and 2.3mm). It works on 24-gauge or thinner metals.

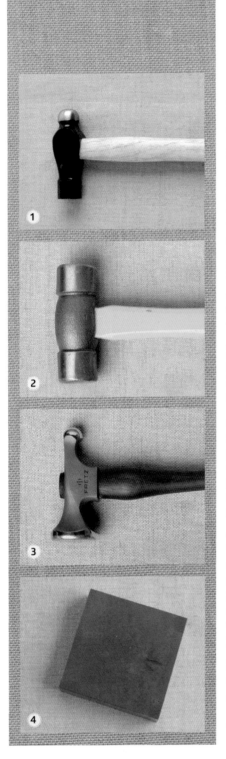

HARDENING, FLATTENING, AND TEXTURING

These tools make soft metals rigid, as well as add patterns or bumps.

metal stamps

Use metal stamps to add text and patterns to metal. Alphabet and number stamps don't have to be used strictly for spelling and math; think of them as basic shapes you can use to create unique patterns.

ball-peen hammer (1)

The round end of the classic hardware-store hammer leaves a textured look on your metal, while the flat end can be used to flatten wire.

brass hammer (2)

Use a one- to three-pound brass hammer with metal stamps to leave deep, even impressions.

chasing hammer (3)

Somewhat similar in look to a ball-peen hammer, the flat end is larger, which means it will cover more surface area when striking. Use the round end to add texture to your metal or for riveting.

texturing hammers

While not essential, these hammers with stripes or circles on the heads can be a fun way to add designs to metal. Some come with interchangeable heads, giving you lots of options without taking up too much space in your studio.

rawhide hammer or plastic mallet

After stamping or texturing, your metal piece might be a little bent out of shape. The rawhide hammer or plastic mallet will help reshape and harden it without leaving any noticeable marks.

bench block or anvil (4)

You'll need a hard steel surface such as a bench block or anvil for hammering. Be sure to place the bench block on a hard surface; a soft surface will absorb some of the force of the hammer and lighten your hammered impressions. Some jewelry makers use a leather sandbag under their bench block to hold it in place and to reduce noise.

SMOOTHING AND HARDENING

These tools remove rough edges or make soft metals rigid.

cup bur

If you make your own ear wires, you'll want to make sure the ends are smooth and comfortable to wear. Insert the wire into the cup and rotate to remove any sharp edges.

files

Metal files smooth rough edges of metal or wire. Always file in the same direction. I like to wear thin work gloves when filing to avoid getting metal splinters in my fingers. Wearing a mask will also ensure that you don't accidentally inhale small metal particles.

tumbler

If you're making your own components such as clasps, ear wires, or jump rings, you'll want a rotary tumbler as well as mixed stainless steel shot to harden and polish your pieces.

COLORING

Patinas, paints, and other materials alter the hue or finish of metal components. You'll need a few simple tools to work with them.

jar or lidded container

Save at least one old empty jar or container with a lid for working with patinas or paints.

paintbrushes, sponges, paper towels

Inexpensive paintbrushes and other tools help decorate your findings.

polishing cloth and steel wool

Give your jewelry a final shine with a polishing cloth. Fine (#0000) steel wool helps remove extra blackening from your piece after being treated with liver of sulfur.

KNOTTING AND SEWING

These tools work with thread, cord, or ribbon.

needles

A beading needle can be helpful for stringing seed beads. Use the point of the needle, rather than your fingers, to pick up the tiny beads from your tray. Use a sewing or embroidery needle to sew the edges of your ribbon to keep it from fraying or to quickly adhere two pieces of fabric, ribbon, or cord together without using glue. A Big Eye needle is the easiest to thread; the "eye" runs the entire length of the needle. Some silk beading cord comes with a needle already attached. When you finish your project, trim the cord as far from the needle as possible so it will be ready for your next use.

clipboard or macramé board

A hard surface with a clamp helps hold your cords in place while you braid or knot.

knotting tweezers ⑤

Use these tweezers to place your knots exactly where you'd like them on your cord. See page 130 in Basic Techniques for instructions.

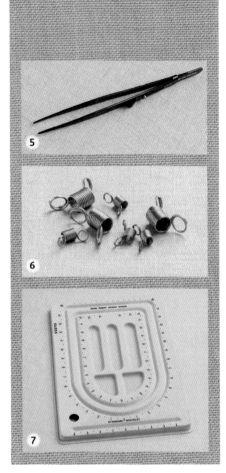

DESIGNING

These tools help you plan the finished look of your jewelry.

bead stops ⑥

These handy spring-like coils can be attached to the ends of in-progress necklaces and bracelets. They're especially valuable for multistrand designs or for absent-minded designers who like to "try on" an unfinished design by holding it up to their neck or draping it over their wrist, forgetting that the clasp hasn't been attached yet. (Been there, done that!)

bead design board or beading mat ⑦

A grooved board with measurements for necklaces and bracelets can be a handy way to visualize your design before stringing. Alternately, a soft beading mat made of velour (or a clean kitchen towel) ensures that your beads do not roll around while you work.

camera

My inexpensive point-and-shoot camera is one of my best design tools. If I cannot take a good photo of a piece, it often means that there's a fundamental problem with it such as an awkwardly hanging pendant or a too-loose clasp. Studying a close-up photo can also alert you to those smaller, easily overlooked details such as an open jump ring or stray wire that can detract from your work.

inspiration book and sketchbook

We've all had those days when we suddenly have free time to create, but no ideas. Take time to save images of nature, home décor, fabric, or other items that inspire you, whether online or in print. A sketchbook or journal can be a handy place to keep track of future project ideas.

neck form, mannequin

Neck forms or mannequins show you how your necklace will look when worn and not flat on your design board.

MEASURING

These tools help determine the size of materials and finished jewelry.

ruler, measuring tape

There's nothing worse than crimping closed a bracelet and then realizing that it's an inch too small for your wrist. Rulers, measuring tapes, and specialized tools, such as a conical bracelet sizer, will ensure that your finished jewelry can be worn by a real person.

digital caliper, wire gauge

If you're the type of beader who visits a shop or a show intending to buy 8mm beads and ends up buying 10mm beads instead, you might want a handheld digital caliper to measure the inside and outside diameter of beads. Similarly, if you tend to remove your wire from neatly labeled packaging, a wire gauge (a metal disc with slits for inserting wires) will help separate the 20-gauge wire from the 22-gauge.

California Poppy

Filigree, satin ribbon, and brass frames stitched together frame a gorgeous handmade lampwork California poppy.

TIP
The interfacing found at fabric stores adds sturdiness to the pendant. If you can't find it, try substituting another thick, stiff material such as leather.

TIP
Making the same number of dangles with each of the three bead types creates a balanced design even if the dangles are added randomly.

MICHELLE MACH

Materials

- 1 orange 24mm lampwork flower
- 12 matte olive green 12×16mm pressed-glass leaves
- 13 orange 3.5–4mm rounds
- 12 iolite 4mm crystal bicones
- 1 silver-plated 4mm round
- 3 brass 12×35mm rectangle filigree connectors
- 2 brass 45mm square frames
- 3" (7.5 cm) of 50mm blue satin ribbon
- 1½" (3.8 mm) of interfacing
- 10" (25.4 cm) of sewing thread
- 4" (10.2 cm) of light brown embroidery floss
- 18" (45.7 cm) of teal embroidery floss
- 25 brass 2" (5.1 cm) head pins
- 12 brass 2" (5.1 cm) eye pins
- 27 brass 4mm jump rings
- 1 brass 7.25mm jump ring
- 1 brass 15mm jump ring
- 1 brass 20×10mm S-clasp
- 18¼" (46.4 cm) of brass 5×8mm ladder chain
- 1" (2.5 cm) of brass 26-gauge craft wire
- Superglue

Tools

Round-nose pliers
2 pairs of chain- or flat-nose pliers
1.8mm metal hole-punch pliers
Wire cutters
Sewing needle
Scissors
Permanent marker

Techniques *(see page 130)*

Jump rings ▪ Overhand knot ▪
Running stitch ▪ Whipstitch ▪
Wrapped loops

Finished Size

19" (48.3 cm)

Variation

Instead of embroidery floss, use 24g wire to wrap the frames together.

1 Use 1 eye pin to center 1 leaf; form a modified briolette-wrapped loop by wrapping the wire to the already formed eye loop. Repeat 11 times to create a total of 12 leaf dangles. Use 1 head pin to string 1 orange round; form a wrapped loop. Repeat 12 times to form a total of 13 orange dangles. Use 1 head pin to string 1 iolite bicone; form a wrapped loop. Repeat 11 times to form a total of 12 bicone dangles.

2 Use the embroidery floss to stitch together the 3 filigree connectors with a running stitch. Line the connectors up vertically and stitch the 4 loops on each side of the middle connector to 4 inner loops of the left and right connectors.

3 Cut the ribbon into two 1½" (3.8 mm) pieces. Stack together the blue satin ribbon piece, the interfacing, the stitched filigree square, the flower, and the silver round. Use the sewing thread to stitch the stack together from the bottom of the ribbon up through the silver bead and back down through the ribbon. Repeat several times. Make sure the stack is tightly stitched together. Tie an overhand knot and dab with glue. Let dry. Set the stack on top of the remaining ribbon piece. Whipstitch the edges of the stack and ribbon together. Tie an overhand knot and dab with glue. Let dry.

4 Using hole-punch pliers, punch 6 holes about ⅛" (3.2 mm) apart along one side of 1 frame. Repeat 3 times to add another 6 holes to each side. Place the frames back to back. Use the marker to mark through the holes in the first frame onto the second frame. Punch 24 holes in the second frame.

5 Insert the ribbon and filigree stack in between the 2 back-to-back frames. Center the stack. Use ½" (1.3 cm) of wire to temporarily bind together the holes aligned in one corner of both frames. Repeat for the pair of holes opposite the first pair. Beginning at one corner, use the teal embroidery floss to sew the 2 frames together using a whipstitch, removing the temporary wire before stitching.

6 String the 15mm jump ring through 1 corner of the frame. Fold the chain in half. Use two 4mm jump rings to attach the 15mm jump ring to the center chain link. Close the 15mm jump ring.

7 Attach the leaf dangles randomly to the chain by opening and closing the eye loop on each as you would a jump ring. Use 4mm jump rings to attach the orange dangles and bicone dangles randomly to the chain. Add more than 1 dangle to a jump ring if you like.

8 Attach the clasp to one end of the chain. Attach the 7.25mm jump ring to the other end of the chain.

Sweet Soirée

Sterling silver bead cones burst with sparkling blue crystals, while handmade bright ceramic rounds form a conga line of color perfect for any celebration.

TIP
Choosing a clasp that matches the cones is an easy way to ensure a cohesive finished design.

LORELEI EURTO

Materials

- 6 red 12mm ceramic rounds
- 4 lime green 12mm ceramic rounds
- 3 teal 12mm ceramic rounds
- 24 Pacific opal 4mm crystal bicones
- 12 turquoise 2×4mm rondelles
- 14 sterling silver 10×7mm willow-print bead cones
- 8 silver-plated 2.5×5mm rondelle spacers
- 36 sterling silver 2" (5.1 cm) head pins
- 2 sterling silver 1×2mm crimp tubes
- 1 sterling silver 25mm willow-print toggle clasp
- 30" (76.2 cm) of silver-colored 22-gauge craft wire
- 9" (22.9 cm) of .019 flexible beading wire

Tools

Round-nose pliers
Crimping pliers
Wire cutters

Techniques *(see page 130)*

Crimping ▪ Stringing ▪ Wrapped loops

Finished Size

9" (22.9 cm)

Variation

Substitute pastel Lucite flowers for the silver cones and add handmade lampwork glass, enamel, and polymer clay beads as Jamie Hogsett does for a lovely version of this project.

1 Use 1 head pin to string 1 crystal bicone; form a wrapped loop. Repeat 23 times for a total of 24 crystal dangles. Repeat with the turquoise rondelles, creating a total of 12 turquoise dangles.

2 Cut the craft wire into 12 pieces, each 2½" (2.5 cm) long. Begin a wrapped loop at one end of 1 wire, attaching 2 crystal dangles and 1 turquoise dangle to the loop before completing the wrap. String 1 bead cone and form a wrapped loop. Repeat with the remaining crystal dangles, turquoise dangles, and bead cones. Set aside.

3 String 1 crimp tube and the toggle bar onto one end of the beading wire. Pass the wire back through the crimp tube and crimp using crimping pliers.

4 String 1 bead cone, 1 red round, and 1 lime green round.

5 String 1 bead cone dangle and 1 spacer; repeat. String 1 bead cone dangle.

6 String 1 teal, 1 red, and 1 lime green round. Repeat Step 5. String 1 red, 1 teal, and 1 red round. Repeat Step 5. String 1 lime, 1 teal, and 1 red round. Repeat Step 5. String 1 lime, 1 red round, and 1 bead cone.

7 String 1 crimp tube and the toggle ring. Pass the wire back through the crimp tube and crimp. Trim any excess wire with wire cutters.

Westward Bound

Foldover cord ends and ribbon ends pair together to form bold Southwestern-inspired leather-fringe earrings.

VARIATION
Use tan leather, red rounds, and silver findings for a brighter look.

ERIN SIEGEL

Materials

- 16 opaque turquoise 6mm glass rounds
- 14 antique brass foldover **cord ends**
- 2 antique brass 1" (2.5 cm) basketweave **ribbon ends**
- 16 antique brass 2" (5.1 cm) head pins
- 2 antique brass leverback ear wires
- 30" (76.2 cm) of black ⅛" (3.2 mm) deerskin leather lace

Tools

Round-nose pliers
Chain-nose pliers
Wire cutters
Scissors
Ruler
2" (5.1 cm) of painter's tape

Techniques *(see page 130)*

Foldover cord ends ▪ Simple loops ▪
Ribbon ends

Finished Size

4½" (11.4 cm)

Tips

Use a piece of painter's tape to keep the leather lace in place while you work.

Instead of cutting the ends off the head pins, use 20 or 22g wire.

Variation

Instead of earrings, create a long, dramatic necklace such as this one by Lorelei Eurto.

1 Cut the leather lace into one 3" (7.6 cm) piece, two 2½" (6.4 cm) pieces, two 2" (5.1 cm) pieces, and two 1½" (3.8 cm) pieces. Set aside.

2 Use 1 head pin to string 1 turquoise round. Trim the wire and form a simple loop. Repeat 6 times for a total of 7 dangles. Set aside.

3 Convert 1 head pin into an eye pin by trimming off the head and forming a simple loop at one end. String 1 turquoise round, trim the wire, and form a simple loop. Set aside.

4 On your work surface, line up the leather strips next to each other in the following order: 1½" (3.8 cm), 2" (5.1 cm), 2½" (6.4 cm), 3" (7.6 cm), 2½" (6.4 cm), 2" (5.1 cm), and 1½" (3.8 cm). Place the piece of painter's tape over the leather strips to keep them in place. Make sure the top ends of the leather strips are even with each other.

5 Insert the even ends of the leather strips into 1 ribbon end and close with chain- or flat-nose pliers. Make sure all the leather strips have been captured securely in the ribbon end.

6 Insert the free end of 1 leather strip into 1 foldover end and close. Repeat 6 times.

7 Attach 1 beaded dangle to the loop of 1 foldover end. Repeat 6 times.

8 Use the bead link from Step 3 to attach the loop on the ribbon end to 1 leverback ear wire.

9 Repeat Steps 1–8 to complete the second earring.

Lotus Blossom

While a real lotus blossom rises from the mud to show off its beauty, the one on this necklace bursts forth from a colorful earring finding.

TIP

Just because a clasp is designed to hold multiple strands, it doesn't mean you need to use all the holes. The empty holes on this box clasp add a decorative touch.

MICHELLE MACH

Materials

- 3 green 8mm 4-hole square shell buttons
- 1 bronze 4mm glass round
- 1 copper-plated 26mm layered lotus
- 1 copper 6mm daisy spacer
- 1 copper 5mm rope spacer
- 1 magenta 33mm vintage Lucite hoop earring finding
- 1 copper 20mm round bezel with scalloped border
- 1 brass 25mm round blank
- 1 copper-plated 8×15mm filigree flower 3-strand box clasp
- 1 copper-plated 2" (5.1 cm) head pin
- 12 copper 4mm jump rings
- 7 copper 6mm jump rings
- 18" (45.7 cm) of olive green 1mm waxed linen cord
- 13" (33 cm) of 3mm copper twisted helix chain

Tools

Round-nose pliers
2 pairs of chain- or flat-nose pliers
Scissors
1.8mm metal hole-punch pliers
Ruler
Permanent marker
Ball-peen or texture hammer (optional)
Bench block (optional)

Techniques *(see page 130)*

Double overhand knots ■ Hole punching ■ Jump rings ■ Simple loops ■ Hammering (optional)

Finished Size

16" (40.6 cm)

Variation

Create an industrial look by combining a black or metal earring hoop, gray cord, black buttons, and a gear.

1 Mark the center of the bezel and punch a hole.

2 Place the bezel inside the Lucite hoop. Use the linen cord to wrap around one side of the hoop twice. Pass the cord through 1 of the nearest loops on the edge of the bezel and out through the adjacent loop on the bezel. Wrap the cord around the hoop again and pass the cord under the bezel to the opposite side of the hoop. Wrap the cord around this side of the hoop twice and attach this side of the bezel as before. Form several double overhand knots below the bezel. Trim.

3 Mark the center of the brass blank and punch a hole. Punch another hole about 2.5mm from the edge of the blank. If desired, hammer the blank for texture. Use the head pin to string the rope spacer, the brass blank, the hole in the bezel, the layered lotus, the daisy spacer, and the bronze round. Form a simple loop, making sure to hold the layers tightly together. Attach a 6mm jump ring to the hole on the edge of the brass blank. Set the pendant aside.

4 Cut the chain into one 8" (20.3 cm) piece and one 5" (12.7 cm) piece. Use one 4mm jump ring to attach the center loop on the filigree half of the clasp to one end of the 8" (20.3 cm) chain. String the pendant. Use one 4mm jump ring to attach the other end of the chain to two 4mm jump rings.

5 Use one 6mm jump ring to attach the previous jump ring pair to 1 hole of 1 button. Use one 6mm jump ring to attach the opposite buttonhole to two 4mm jump rings. Repeat the entire step twice. Use one 4mm jump ring to attach the last jump ring pair to one end of the 5" (12.7 cm) chain. Use one 4mm jump ring to attach the other end of the chain to the middle loop on the other half of the clasp.

Retro Mix

Connect slide-lock clasps to create a long
necklace in a retro palette of bright orange,
green, gray, and gold or disconnect them for
a bold choker and bracelet set.

JAMIE HOGSETT

Materials

- 1 gray with white/purple/orange/green details 23mm lampwork-glass focal round
- 16 gray 6mm pressed-glass rounds
- 18 orange 6mm pressed-glass rounds
- 14 orange moonlight–lined striped 8mm vintage Lucite rounds
- 8 green 8mm Lucite rounds
- 5 assorted green 9×3–9×7mm lampwork-glass discs
- 2 assorted orange 11×8–13×8mm lampwork-glass rondelles
- 1 orange with white dots 12×9mm lampwork-glass rondelle
- 20 gold-plated pewter 6×4mm faceted gold rondelles
- 8 jade 6mm crystal pearls
- 8 ivory 6mm crystal pearls
- 16 dark purple 4mm crystal pearls
- 4 gold-plated pewter 6mm bull's-eye coins
- 111 (about ½ gram) dark purple size 14° seed beads (A)
- 172 (about 5 grams) silver gray Ceylon pearl size 8° seed beads (B)
- 24 gold 2" (5.1 cm) eye pins
- 18 copper 2mm crimp tubes
- 18 gold-filled 3mm crimp covers
- 1 gold vermeil 18×21mm etched toggle clasp
- 2 gold-plated 3-strand slide-lock clasps
- 4" (10.2 cm) of gold-plated 24-gauge wire
- 87" (2.2 m) of 14k gold .019 flexible beading wire
- 20" (50.8 cm) of gold-plated 5×6mm oval chain

Tools

Round-nose pliers ▪ 2 pairs of chain- or flat-nose pliers ▪ Crimping pliers ▪ Nylon-jaw pliers ▪ Wire cutters ▪ Bead stops

Techniques *(see page 130)*

Crimping ▪ Crimp covers ▪ Stringing ▪ Wrapped loops

Finished Size

23" (58.4 cm) necklace; 7" (17.8 cm) or bracelet and 16" (40.6 cm) choker

CHOKER

1 Cut the chain into six 3¼" (8.3 cm) pieces. Set aside.

2 Use 1 eye pin to string 1 orange striped round. Wrap the wire down around the bead and coil it around the eye pin between the eye and the bead. Repeat 5 times.

3 Repeat Step 2 using orange glass rounds, gray rounds, and purple pearls. Set aside 4 orange striped dangles, 4 purple pearl dangles, 4 orange glass dangles, and 2 gray dangles. Mix the remaining dangles together.

4 Use 9" (22.9 cm) of flexible beading wire to string 1 crimp tube and the first loop of outer half of a slide-lock clasp. Pass back through the tube; crimp and cover. String 1 of the dangles formed in Steps 2 and 3, 1A, 1B, 1 dangle, 1A, 1B, 1 green Lucite round, 1B, 1 gold rondelle, 1B, 1 orange striped round, 1B, 1A, 1B, 1 ivory pearl, 1B, 1A, 1B, 1 gray round, 1B, 1A, 1B, 1 orange glass round, 1B, 1 gold rondelle, 1B, 1 jade pearl, 1B, 1A, 1B, 1 purple pearl, 1B, 1A, 1B, 1A, 1 crimp tube, and the end of 1 chain piece. Pass back through the tube; crimp and cover.

5 Use 9" (22.9 cm) of flexible beading wire to string 1 crimp tube and the second loop of outer half of the remaining slide clasp. Pass back through the tube; crimp and cover. String 1 dangle (formed in Steps 2 and 3), 1A, 1B, 1 dangle, 1A, 1B, 1 green round, 1B, 1A, 1B, 1 orange striped round, 1B, 1 gold rondelle, 1B, 1 ivory pearl, 1B, 1A, 1B, 1 gray round, 1B, 1 gold rondelle, 1B, 1 orange glass round, 1B, 1A, 1B, 1 jade pearl, 1B, 1 gold rondelle, 1B, 1 purple pearl, 1B, 1A, 1B, 1 crimp tube, and the end of 1 chain piece. Pass back through the tube; crimp and cover.

6 Use 9" (22.9 cm) of flexible beading wire to string 1 crimp tube and the third loop of outer half of the remaining slide clasp. Pass back through the tube; crimp and cover. String 1 dangle (formed in Steps 2 and 3), 1A, 1B, 1 dangle, 1A, 1B, 1 green round, 1B, 1A, 1B, 1 orange striped round, 1B, 1A, 1B, 1 ivory pearl, 1B, 1 gold rondelle, 1B, 1 gray round, 1B, 1A, 1B, 1 orange glass round, 1B, 1A, 1B, 1 jade pearl, 1B, 1A, 1B, 1 purple pearl, 1B, 1 gold rondelle, 1B, 1A, 1 crimp tube, and the end of 1 chain piece. Pass back through the tube; crimp and cover.

7 Use 2" (5.1 cm) of gold-plated wire to form a wrapped loop that attaches to the other ends of the 3 chain pieces used in Steps 4–6. String 1 orange glass round; form a wrapped loop that attaches to one half of the toggle clasp.

8 Repeat Steps 4–7 for the other half of the choker, using the inner half of the slide clasp and the remaining half of the toggle clasp.

9 Open the eye pins on the dangles set aside in Step 3. Attach 1 orange striped dangle and 1 purple pearl dangle to the first loop on the outside half of the slide clasp, with the beaded strand in the middle of the dangles. Repeat on the third loop of the slide clasp. Attach 1 gray dangle and 1 orange glass dangle to the second loop on the slide clasp, with the beaded strand between the dangles. Repeat this entire step on the inside half of the slide clasp.

BRACELET

1 Use 11" (27.9 cm) of flexible beading wire to string 1 crimp tube and the first loop of the outside half of 1 slide clasp; pass back through the tube and crimp. Cover the tube with 1 crimp cover. String {1 size 14° seed bead (A) and 1 size 8° seed bead (B)} twice. String 1 green disc, 1B, 1 orange glass round, 1B, 1A, 3B, 1A, 1 ivory pearl, and 1A. String {1B and 1A} three times. String 1 purple pearl. String {1A and 1B} twice. String 1 orange rondelle, 1B and 1A. String 1 gold rondelle, the focal round, and 1 gold rondelle. String {1A and 1B} twice. String 1 orange glass round and 1A. String {2B and 1A} twice. String 1B, 1 green round, 1B, 1A, and 1 gold coin. String {1A and 1B} twice. String the orange with white dots rondelle. String 1B, 1A, 2B, 1A, 1 gray round, 1A, 1 purple pearl, 1A, and 1 crimp tube. Place a bead stop on the end of the wire and set aside.

TIP

Keep the halves of the slide clasp together when crimping wires to the clasp(s) to ensure that you're connecting the correct wires to the correct half of the clasp.

Variation

Rather than making a choker and a bracelet, make three bracelets that can be combined into one necklace.

2 Use 11" (27.9 cm) of flexible beading wire to string 1 crimp tube and the second loop of the outside half of the slide clasp; pass back through the tube and crimp. Cover the tube with 1 crimp cover. String {1A and 1B} three times. String 1 gold coin, 1B, 1A, 1B, 1 orange striped round, 1B, 1A, 1 gray round, 1 green disc, 1B, 1A, 1B, 1 green round, 1B, 1A, 3B, and 1A. Pass through the gold rondelle, focal round, and gold rondelle at the center of the previous strand. String 1A, 3B, 1A, 1B, 1 gold rondelle, 1 green disc, 1 gold rondelle, 1B, 1A, 1B, 1 orange striped round, 1B, 1A, 1 ivory pearl, 1A, 1B, 1 purple pearl, 1B, 1 green rondelle, 1B, 1A, 3B, 1A, 1B, 1A, and 1 crimp tube. Place a bead stop on the end of the wire and set aside.

3 Use 11" (27.9 cm) of flexible beading wire to string 1 crimp tube and the third loop of the outside half of the slide clasp; pass back through the tube and crimp. Cover the tube with 1 crimp cover. String 1A, 1 gray round, 1 purple pearl, 1A, 1B, 1 gold rondelle, 1 orange rondelle, 1 gold rondelle, 1B, 1A, 2B, 1A, 1 jade pearl, 1A, 1B, 1 gold coin, and 1A. String {1B and 1A} twice. String 1 orange glass round, 1A, 1B, and 1A. Pass through the gold rondelle, focal round, and gold rondelle at the center of the previous strand. String 1A, 1B, 1A, 1 gray round, and 1A. String {1B and 1A} three times. String 1 jade pearl. String {1A and 1B} three times. String 1 gold coin. String {1A and 1B} twice. String 1 green disc. String {1B and 1A} four times. String 1 orange round. String {1B and 1A} three times. String 1 crimp tube.

4 Place the 3 open strands next to each other and add or subtract seed beads if necessary to ensure equal lengths. Use the strand without the bead stop to string the opposite loop of the inner half of the clasp. Pass back through the tube; crimp and cover. Remove the bead stop from the wire used in Step 2 and string the opposite loop of the inner half of the clasp. Pass back through the tube; crimp and cover. Repeat to attach the remaining wire to the remaining loop of the clasp.

Two to Tango

Rather than hiding under beads in beaded links,
unadorned eye pins enjoy their moment of glory
in these swingy fan-shaped earrings.

TIP

If you make your
own eye pins or trim
commercially made ones,
use a cup bur tool to
round and smooth the
wire tips to ensure
a comfortable,
nonlethal fit.

MICHELLE MACH

Materials

- 2 red 18×6mm ceramic discs
- 2 yellow 8×6mm fire-polished glass rondelles
- 4 brass 5mm daisy spacers
- 28 brass 1½" (3.8 cm) eye pins
- 4 brass 4mm jump rings
- 2 brass 10mm jump rings
- 2 brass ear wires

Tools

Round-nose pliers
2 pairs of chain- or flat-nose pliers
Wire cutters

Techniques (see page 130)

Jump rings ■ Simple loops ■ Wrapped loops

Finished Size

3½" (8.9 cm)

"Keep a notebook of your design ideas. Even if you never make them, it's comforting to know you have pages of inspiration waiting for you if you ever feel blocked."
—Michelle Mach

1 Use 1 eye pin to string 1 daisy spacer, 1 red disc, 1 yellow rondelle, and 1 daisy spacer; form a wrapped loop. Use two 4mm jump rings to attach the top loop of the beaded link to 1 ear wire.

2 Use one 10mm jump ring to string 13 eye pins. Attach the jump ring to the bottom loop of the beaded link.

3 Repeat Steps 1–2 for the second earring.

Variation

Combine turquoise pressed-glass, carved wood tubes, and a domed 3-to-1 brass connector for a Bohemian look. Use a permanent marker to mark the places to cut the eye pins so that they form a graduated curve.

Central Spark

Create a striking geometric pendant for a modern necklace by nesting bead frames within bead frames.

TIP

In a hurry? Use a purchased clasp and jump rings instead of making your own.

CINDY WIMMER

Materials

- 3 crystal 4mm bicones
- 2 gold-and-crystal 6×2mm rondelles
- 140 brass 2×3mm cornerless cubes
- 1 sterling silver 25mm **bead frame**
- 1 sterling silver 17mm **bead frame**
- 1 sterling silver 11mm **bead frame**
- 2 gold-plated 2mm crimp tubes
- 6" (15.2 cm) of 20-gauge red brass wire
- 6½" (16.5 cm) of 16-gauge sterling silver wire
- 20" (50.8 cm) of .015 gold satin flexible beading wire

Tools

Round-nose pliers
Chain-nose pliers
Flat-nose pliers
Crimping pliers
6mm bail-making pliers
Stepped pliers or 5mm mandrel
Wire cutters
Flat file

Techniques *(see page 130)*

Coiling ▪ Crimping ▪ Double-wrapped loops ▪ Jump rings ▪ Spirals ▪ Stringing

Finished Size

17" (43.2 cm)

"A practice spool of copper wire and a few simple tools can provide all the inspiration you need."
—Cindy Wimmer

1 Use 3" (7.6 cm) of sterling silver wire to create a clasp. Grasp one end of the wire with the back of your round-nose pliers and make a loop. Hold the loop flat in the jaws of your flat-nose pliers and use your fingers to coil the wire around the loop once to form a spiral. Grasp the other end of the wire with the 6mm jaw of the bail-making pliers and form a loop facing in the opposite direction, creating the hook end of the clasp. Trim the wire and file the end smooth.

2 Coil the remaining sterling silver wire around the 5mm barrel of the stepped pliers and then cut the coil into 4 jump rings. Open 1 jump ring and attach it to 2 more jump rings, forming a chain; set aside. Attach the remaining jump ring to the spiral on the clasp.

3 Make a small loop on the tip of the red brass wire with your round-nose pliers. Squeeze the loop with flat-nose pliers to flatten it. Bend the tail up so that it is perpendicular and string the 11mm bead frame, 1 crystal rondelle, the 17mm bead frame, 1 crystal rondelle, and the 25mm bead frame.

4 Make a double-wrapped loop at the top of the bead-frame pendant, using the back of your round-nose pliers to form the loop.

5 Use the flexible beading wire to string 1 crimp tube and the jump ring on the clasp. Pass the wire back through the tube and crimp the tube with crimping pliers. String 8⅝" (21.9 cm) of brass cubes. String 1 bicone and 3 brass cubes twice, ending with 1 bicone. String 5½" (14 cm) of brass cubes after the last bicone. Slide the bead frame pendant over the brass cubes. String 1 crimp tube and one end of the jump ring in the jump ring-chain from Step 2. Pass the wire back through the tube and crimp.

Variation

Michelle Mach combined peridot and white framelike shells, amethyst crystals, and silver-plated bead frames for lightweight, swingy earrings.

Dancing Damselfly

With the touch of a metal hole punch, an ornate dragonfly becomes a beautiful bail for a handmade ceramic pendant. To finish this earthy necklace, combine a diamond-shaped filigree and a 2-hole connector to form a unique clasp.

TIP

Waxed threaded knots are extremely difficult to undo. Even if you can, you'll leave behind kinked thread. Be sure you have a snug fit against the bead before you tighten the knot. Use chain-nose pliers or tweezers to move the knot up or down the strand before tightening.

DENISE YEZBAK MOORE

Materials

- 1 lime 35mm ceramic lotus-flower pendant
- 1 brass 50×39mm ornate dragonfly
- 1 green 5×13mm ceramic rondelle
- 1 green 6×7mm ceramic rondelle
- 1 green 6×9mm ceramic rondelle
- 1 green 7×9mm ceramic rondelle
- 1 tan 9×11mm ceramic rondelle
- 1 lime 7×9mm ceramic rondelle
- 1 lime 9×10mm ceramic rondelle
- 1 lime/tan 10×13mm ceramic rondelle
- 1 flower 11×15mm ceramic rondelle
- 1 dark brown 10mm ceramic round
- 1 polka dot 14×17mm ceramic oval
- 1 green 11×11mm ceramic oval
- 1 lime 12×13mm ceramic oval
- 1 brass 64×21mm trellis diamond filigree connector
- 1 brass 19×9mm 2-hole nouveau swirls link/connector
- 1 brass 15mm jump ring
- 1 brass 4mm jump ring
- 94" (2.4 m) of walnut brown 7-cord linen thread
- Superglue

Tools

Round-nose pliers
2 pairs of chain- or flat-nose pliers
Wire cutters
1.8mm metal hole-punch pliers
3mm/5mm bail-making pliers
Scissors
Ruler

Techniques (see page 130)

Coiling ▪ Filigree forming ▪ Gluing ▪ Hole punching ▪ Jump rings ▪ Knotting with tweezers ▪ Overhand knots ▪ Simple loops ▪ Stringing

Finished Size

18½" (47 cm)

Note: *All the knots in this project will be overhand knots.*

1 Using the hole-punch pliers, punch a hole in the top left and top right corner of the upper dragonfly wings.

2 Use round-nose pliers to form a simple loop with the dragonfly tail and attach the lotus pendant to the loop. Reinsert the round-nose pliers into the simple loop and continue rotating the pliers to form a 2½-loop coil.

3 Use the 3mm jaw of the bail-making pliers to gently bend the nouveau swirl filigree into a U shape. Slip the 15mm jump ring onto the U shape and connect the 2 holes of the nouveau swirl with the 4mm jump ring.

4 Use wire cutters to cut across the center of the diamond trellis filigree connector creating 2 separate filigree pieces. Grasp the pointed tip of 1 filigree piece, ½" (1.3 cm) from the point, with the 5mm jaw of the bail-making pliers. Gently bend the filigree into a hook. (Save the other half for a future project.)

5 Cut 47" (1.2 m) of linen thread and string the hole in the left wing of the dragonfly. Center the thread in the hole and use both strands to form an overhand knot.

6 String the lime 9×10mm rondelle and form an overhand knot. String the dark brown round and form a knot. Move up the thread ½" (1.3 cm) and form a knot. String the lime ceramic 7×9mm rondelle, knot, move up ½" (1.3 cm) and knot. String the green 11×11mm oval, knot, move up ½" (1.3 cm) and knot. String the polka dot oval, knot, move up ½" (1.3 cm) and knot. String the tan 9×11mm rondelle, knot, move up ½" (1.3 cm) and knot. String the green 5×13mm rondelle and knot. Move up ½" (1.3 cm) and form a knot; repeat twice. String the 4mm jump ring from Step 3 and knot.

7 Trim the thread tail to ¾" (1.9 cm) and fray the ends. Dab the last knot with superglue to secure. Let dry.

8 Using the remaining piece of linen thread, string the hole in the right wing of the dragonfly. Center the thread in the hole, bring strands together, and form a knot.

9 Move up ½" (1.3 cm) and form a knot. String the flower rondelle, knot, move up ½" (1.3 cm) and knot. String the green 6×9mm rondelle, knot, move up ½" (1.3 cm) and knot. String the lime/tan rondelle, knot, move up ½" (1.3 cm) and knot. String the green 7×9mm rondelle, knot, move up ½" (1.3 cm) and knot. String the lime 12×13mm oval, knot, move up ½" (1.3 cm) and knot. String the green 6×7mm rondelle and knot. Move up ½" (1.3 cm) and knot; repeat once.

10 Separate the strands and use 1 strand to string the left bottom hole of the filigree hook from Step 4; form 3 knots. Trim this thread and dab the knot with superglue to secure. String the other strand through the right bottom hole of the filigree hook, form 3 knots, trim the thread, and glue the knot. Let dry.

May
Flowers

Sweet filigree ring bands turn into
earrings reminiscent of overflowing
flower baskets, the kind you might
see hanging from Southern front
porches in the summer.

VARIATION

Use green glass leaves,
copper rounds, and
yellow and orange Lucite
calla lilies. Because the
wrapped loops are the
same size as the bead
holes, these dangles
have less movement
than the other pair.

MICHELLE MACH

Materials

- 12 blue-gray 12mm Lucite 6-petal flowers
- 4 clear 4mm crystal bicones
- 4 amethyst 4mm crystal bicones
- 4 magenta 5mm crystal bicones
- 8 white 4mm crystal pearls
- 2 brass filigree ring bands
- 20 brass 26-gauge 2" (5.1 cm) head pins
- 2 brass 15mm jump rings
- 4 brass 4mm jump rings
- 2 brass 7mm jump rings
- 2 brass ear wires

Tools

Round-nose pliers
2 pairs chain- or flat-nose pliers
Wire cutters

Techniques *(see page 130)*

Jump rings ■ Wrapped loops

Finished Size

2" (5.1 cm)

Tip

Look for ring bands created with brass, rather than brass-coated steel, to create long-lasting jewelry. (Steel rusts when wet!)

"Save one of your early jewelry designs and look at it every year. There's no better way to see how far you've come!"
—Michelle Mach

1 Use 1 head pin to string 1 crystal bicone; form a small wrapped loop that is just large enough to go over the 15mm jump ring. Repeat 11 times to create a total of 12 crystal bicone dangles. Use 1 head pin to string 1 pearl; form a wrapped loop. Repeat 7 times to create a total of 8 pearl dangles.

2 Use one 15mm jump ring to string the ends of the ring band.

3 String 1 pearl dangle through the hole in 1 flower. String the pearl/flower dangle on the jump ring.

4 String 1 clear crystal bicone through the hole in 1 flower. String the crystal/flower dangle on the jump ring. Repeat Step 3. String 1 magenta bicone dangle and 1 amethyst bicone dangle on the jump ring.

5 Repeat Steps 3–4 in reverse order and close the jump ring.

6 Use one 7mm jump ring to connect the 15mm jump ring to one 4mm jump ring, making sure to attach the 7mm jump ring in between the 2 amethyst dangles. Use one 4mm jump ring to attach the previous 4mm jump ring to 1 ear wire.

7 Repeat Steps 2–6 for the second earring.

Tip

Instead of using ring bands, you can use a diamond-shaped filigree connector and bend it into a circular ring shape using a ring mandrel, large bail-making pliers, or a metal pipe.

Fringe Benefits

Two vintage coral gemasite box clasps form an innovative focal piece for this elegant necklace. With a simple click of a clasp, rearrange the focal piece to form four different looks

TIP

Make sure that both box clasps for the focal piece have identically sized and shaped tabs and slots. Otherwise, they won't be interchangeable.

ERIN PRAIS-HINTZ

Materials

- 196 dyed coral bamboo 6×3mm dog bones
- 44 silver lustre 10mm glass coins
- 2 vintage coral gemasite 33×29mm silver-filled 5-strand box clasps
- 1 vintage coral gemasite 26×11.5mm silver-filled box clasp
- 2 silver-plated 8mm jump rings
- 13 silver-plated 5mm jump rings
- 7 silver-plated 4mm jump rings
- 11 silver-plated 2mm crimp tubes
- 37" (94 cm) of .018 flexible beading wire
- 13" (33 cm) of silver-plated 2.8mm flattened cable chain

Tools

2 pairs of chain- or flat-nose pliers
Crimping pliers
Wire cutters

Techniques *(see page 130)*

Crimping ▪ Jump rings ▪ Stringing

Finished Size

16" (40.6 cm)

Variation

Attach a single, small filigree box clasp to a filigree ring adorned with magenta pressed-glass flowers to create the focal for Michelle Mach's version of this necklace. By attaching the green glass leaves to the bottom half of the clasp, you can remove them on days you'd prefer an even simpler look.

1 Cut the flexible beading wire into the following pieces: two 9" (22.9 cm) and two 9½" (24.1 cm).

2 Use a 9" (22.9 cm) piece of flexible beading wire to string 1 crimp tube and the second loop from one end of the box-side of 1 large box clasp (clasp A). Pass the wire back through the tube and crimp the tube with crimping pliers. String 98 bamboo dog bones, 1 crimp tube, and one 8mm jump ring. Pass the wire back through the tube and crimp. Repeat this entire step on the second loop from the opposite end.

3 Use a 9½" (24.1 cm) piece of flexible beading wire to string 1 crimp tube and the outside loop on one end of the box-side of clasp A. String 22 coin beads, 1 crimp tube, and the 8mm jump ring from Step 2, making sure this strand is on the outside of the previous strand. Pass the wire back through the tube and crimp. Repeat this entire step on the outside loop on the opposite end.

4 Use three 4mm jump rings to attach the 8mm jump ring from Step 2 to half of the small box clasp. Repeat, attaching the 8mm jump ring from Step 3 to the remaining half of this clasp.

5 Remove the clasp tab (tab A) from clasp A. Use one 4mm jump ring to attach the middle loop of tab A to the middle loop of the box-side of the second large box clasp (clasp B). Repeat using 5mm jump rings to attach the remaining loops on tab A to the corresponding loops on the box-side of clasp B.

6 Cut the chain into the following pieces: 2" (5.1 cm), two 1" (2.5 cm), two 1¼" (3.2 cm), two 1½" (3.8 cm), and two 1¾" (4.4 cm).

7 Remove the clasp tab (tab B) from clasp B. Use one 5mm jump ring to attach each of the following: the 2" (5.1 cm) chain to the center loop on tab B, the two 1½" (3.8 cm) chains to the loops on either side of the center loop, and the two 1" (2.5 cm) chains to the outermost loops.

8 Use one 5mm jump ring to attach a 1¼" (3.2 cm) chain to the 2 outermost jump rings on one end. Repeat on the opposite end.

9 Use one 5mm jump ring to attach a 1¾" (4.4 cm) chain to the jump rings attached to the center loop and the loop to the left of the center. Repeat with the center loop and the loop to the right of center.

Hanawa

Create a colorful garland of flowers with ribbon ends and Japanese floral crepe cords. *Hanawa* means "garland" in Japanese.

TIP

Stretch your beading budget by using pretty floral novelty chain only in the front of your necklace and less expensive cord at the back.

LORELEI EURTO

Materials

- 14" (35.6 cm) of 4–6mm floral crepe cord
- 23" (58.4 cm) of 3mm teal suede lace
- 8 copper 13mm basketweave ribbon ends
- 1 brass 5×10mm foldover cord end
- 2 brass 4mm jump rings
- 8 brass 7mm jump rings
- 1 copper 28mm sunflower hook clasp
- 10" (25.4 cm) of brass 10mm flower-fringe chain

Tools

2 pairs of chain- or flat-nose pliers
Scissors

Techniques *(see page 130)*

Foldover cord ends ■ Jump rings ■ Overhand knot ■ Ribbon ends

Finished Size

22" (55.8 cm)

Variation

Instead of creating a garland with equal-length ribbons, begin with a large loop in the center and make gradually smaller loops on either side.

1 Fold the suede cord in half. Tie an overhand knot at the folded end, leaving enough of a loop to hook onto the hook clasp. Attach a foldover cord end to both strands on the opposite end of the suede lace.

2 Use one 4mm jump ring to attach the foldover cord end to one end of the chain.

3 Use scissors to cut the floral crepe cord into 7 pieces, each 2" (5.1 cm) long.

4 Attach 1 ribbon end to one end of a crepe cord; close the ribbon end with chain- or flat-nose pliers. Attach another ribbon end to the other end of the crepe cord, plus one end of a second crepe cord and close. Repeat this step with the remaining crepe cords and ribbon ends.

5 Attach one 7mm jump ring to each of the ribbon ends and attach each jump ring along the chain length at 1½" (3.8 cm) intervals.

6 Use a 4mm jump ring to attach the clasp to the free end of the chain.

Leaves of Gold

Instead of hiding a single glue-on bail at the back of your pendant, use multiple rich gold bails as decorative drops. A handmade button clasp adds the perfect finishing touch.

TIP

Use a pair of round-nose pliers to smooth rough spots and clean out the inside of the wood beads for easier stringing.

ERIN SIEGEL

Materials

- 24 sodalite 6mm rounds
- 24 dark brown 12mm ribbed wood rounds
- 1,389 (about 40 grams) Czech opaque olive matte AB size 8° seed beads
- 12 gold-plated 24×10mm leaf bails
- 1 gold-tone 20mm 4-hole button
- 78' (23.8 m) of orange 4-ply Irish waxed linen cord

Tools

Round-nose pliers (optional)
Scissors
Ruler

Techniques *(see page 130)*

Overhand knots ▪ Square knot ▪ Stringing

Finished Size

30" (76.2 cm)

Variation

Instead of using multiple strands of linen, string smaller beads and bails on a single strand of flexible beading wire for a simpler look.

"Practice is the only thing that will get you good and comfortable with jewelry making."
—Erin Siegel

1 Cut the linen cord into six 13" (33 cm) pieces. Align the cords and hold them together at their centers. Twist the centers of the cords tightly together for 3" (7.6 cm). Fold the cords in half and form an overhand knot 1" (2.5 cm) from the fold, creating a loop of twisted cord.

2 Use 6 cords to string 1 wood round; use all 12 cords to form an overhand knot. Repeat this 11 times.

3 Use 1 cord to string 122 seed beads (about 8½" [21.6 cm]). Repeat 10 times. Use the remaining cord to string 7 seed beads. String {1 sodalite round, 1 leaf bail, 1 sodalite round, and 3 seed beads}; repeat 10 times. String 1 sodalite round, 1 leaf bail, 1 sodalite round, and 7 seed beads. Use all 12 cords to form an overhand knot.

4 Repeat Step 2.

5 Use 3 cords to string 1 buttonhole; repeat 3 times to string the remaining buttonholes. Use all 12 cords to form a square knot on top of the button. Trim the cord ends to ¼" (6.4 mm).

Gypsy Girl

Snap clasps turn pretty paillettes into decorative dangles in this bright gemstone and glass bracelet.

TIP

Using two paillettes instead of one not only lets you make a reversible bracelet, but also strengthens the paillettes and makes them less likely to bend. Glue the paillettes together with the holes aligned if you want to strengthen the connection.

MICHELLE MACH

Materials

- 6 silver 20mm paisley embossed plastic paillettes
- 6 teal 20mm paisley embossed plastic paillettes
- 3 teal 10mm pressed-glass coins
- 16 pink crazy lace agate 6×4mm faceted rondelles
- 16 teal 4×3mm faceted-glass rondelles
- 5 magenta 6×4mm faceted-glass rondelles
- 3 matte teal 6×2mm glass rondelles
- 9 gunmetal 6mm melon rounds
- 3 teal 9×6mm pressed-glass flowers
- 2 teal 8mm sequins
- 6 gunmetal 8×12mm snap clasps
- 1 gunmetal 7×12mm lobster clasp
- 22 gunmetal ball-end 2" (5.1 cm) head pins
- 9 gunmetal 2" (5.1 cm) eye pins
- 38 assorted gunmetal and black 4–6mm jump rings
- 1 gunmetal 8mm jump ring
- 5½" (14 cm) of gunmetal etched 5×9mm/4×3mm oval chain
- Jeweler's glue (optional)

Tools

Round-nose pliers
2 pairs of chain- or flat-nose pliers
Wire cutters
Scissors
⅛" (3mm) paper hole punch

Techniques (see page 130)

Jump rings ■ Simple loops ■ Wrapped loops

Finished size

8" (20.3 cm)

Tip

To utilize a too-short piece of chain, add one or two beaded links to the end of the chain to reach the desired length.

1 Use 1 head pin to string 1 teal coin; form a wrapped loop. Repeat twice. Use 1 head pin to string 1 teal flower; form a wrapped loop. Repeat twice. Use 1 head pin to string 3 teal rondelles; form a wrapped loop. Repeat twice. Use 1 head pin to string 1 matte teal rondelle and 1 magenta rondelle; form a wrapped loop. Repeat twice. Use 1 head pin to string 2 pink lace agate rondelles; form a wrapped loop. Repeat 3 times. Use 1 head pin to string 1 melon round and 1 pink lace agate rondelle; form a wrapped loop. Use 1 head pin to string 1 pink lace agate rondelle and 1 melon round; form a wrapped loop. Use 1 head pin to string 1 magenta rondelle; form a wrapped loop. Repeat twice. Use 1 eye pin to string 2 pink lace agate rondelles; form a wrapped loop. Use 1 eye pin to string 1 melon round and 1 pink lace agate rondelle; form a wrapped loop. Repeat. Use 1 eye pin to string 1 pink lace agate rondelle and 1 melon round; form a wrapped loop. Repeat. Use 1 eye pin to string 1 teal rondelle and 1 teal sequin; form a wrapped loop. Repeat. Use 1 eye pin to string 3 teal rondelles; form a simple loop. Use 1 eye pin to string 2 teal rondelles; form a simple loop. Use 1 eye pin to string 2 melon rounds; form a simple loop.

2 Using the paper hole punch, punch a hole over the existing paillette hole of 1 silver paillette. Repeat with 1 teal paillette. Place both paillettes over the ball half of the snap clasp and secure snugly. Place the socket part of the clasp on top of the paillettes and close. Repeat this entire step 5 times to create a total of 6 paillette dangles. Set aside.

3 Use one 5mm jump ring to attach the lobster clasp to one end of the double melon-round link. Use one 5mm jump ring to attach the other end of the link to one end of the chain. Attach one 8mm jump ring to the other end of the chain.

4 Mix the beaded dangles and paillette dangles together. Use 1 jump ring to attach 1 dangle to 1 link in the chain. Repeat, attaching 1–3 dangles to each chain link.

Botanica

Show off your favorite bead
treasures by hanging them from
an oversized lobster clasp.

LORELEI EURTO

Materials

- 1 green 38×10mm lampwork-glass tube
- 1 pink 8×12mm lampwork-glass rondelle
- 6 copper 10×15mm flat ovals
- 194 (about 6 grams) pink purple luster 2×4mm peanut seed beads
- 4 green 12×8mm glass briolettes
- 1 tin 10×20mm coin
- 1 pink 5×10mm enameled flower bead cap
- 1 brass 6mm scalloped bead cap
- 2 brass 12mm filigree bead caps
- 1 pink 5mm ball-end lampwork-glass head pin
- 1 pink 18×20mm lampwork-glass flower head pin
- 1 green 10×20mm lampwork-glass drop head pin
- 5 copper 6mm jump rings
- 2 copper 2mm crimp tubes
- 1 copper 18×40mm swivel lobster clasp
- 20" (50.8 cm) of .019 flexible beading wire

Tools

Round-nose pliers
2 pairs of chain- or flat-nose pliers
Crimping pliers
Wire cutters

Techniques *(see page 130)*

Crimping ▪ Jump rings ▪ Stringing ▪ Wrapped loops

Finished Size

19½" (49.5 cm)

1 Use the pink lampwork ball-end head pin to string the scalloped bead cap and the green lampwork tube bead. Form a wrapped loop. Use one 6mm jump ring to attach the wrapped loop to the ring on the lobster clasp. Use the pink flower head pin to string 1 filigree bead cap. Form a wrapped loop. Use one 6mm jump ring to attach this loop to the right of the tube bead. Use the green lampwork drop head pin to string 1 filigree bead cap. Form a wrapped loop. Use one 6mm jump ring to attach this loop to the left of the tube bead.

2 String 1 crimp tube and one 6mm jump ring onto one end of the beading wire. Pass the wire back through the crimp tube and crimp using crimping pliers.

3 String 1 copper oval bead and 2 peanut seed beads. Repeat 4 times. String 184 (or about 13" [33 cm]) peanut seed beads.

4 String the enameled flower bead cap so the open bloom points toward the peanut seed beads. String 1 pink rondelle, 4 green glass briolettes, 1 tin coin, and 1 copper oval bead.

5 String 1 crimp tube and one 6mm jump ring. Pass the wire back through the crimp tube and crimp.

6 Attach the 6mm jump rings on the beaded necklace to the jaw of the lobster clasp.

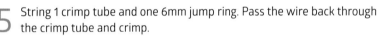

Variation

In Erin Siegel's necklace, the dangles hang from the part of a spring-ring clasp that opens, making it easy to swap out the dangles on a whim.

Meditation Garden

Link hammered toggle rings and leafy toggle bars to create a soothing bracelet that's smooth against your skin and gentle on the soul.

VARIATION
Skip the toggle bars and connect only the rings for a playful version in shades of green, blue, and gold.

JAMIE HOGSETT

Materials

- 2 cream-and-brown 12×7mm polymer clay rondelles
- 2 cream-and-green 12×7mm polymer clay rondelles
- 2 silver 19mm bamboo etched aluminum discs
- 1 brass 17mm dragonfly link
- 1 brass 38×24mm leaf **toggle ring**
- 2 brass 21mm hammered round **toggle rings**
- 2 brass 18mm etched square **toggle rings**
- 2 brass 6×30mm leaf **toggle bars**
- 1 brass 5×30mm engraved **toggle bar**
- 2 silver 2mm ball-end 2" (5.1 cm) head pins
- 1 silver 6mm flower-end 2" (5.1 cm) head pin
- 24" (61 cm) of non-tarnish silver 24-gauge wire
- 3" (7.6 cm) of brass 4×5mm unsoldered etched oval chain (21 links)
- Superglue

Tools

Round-nose pliers
2 pairs of chain- or flat-nose pliers
2 pairs of nylon-jaw pliers
1.8mm metal hole-punch pliers
Wire cutters
Permanent marker
Nylon-jaw ring bending pliers (optional)

Techniques *(see page 130)*

Double-wrapped loops ▪ Gluing ▪ Hole punching ▪ Jump rings ▪ Wire wrapping ▪ Wrapped loops

Finished Size

7½" (19.1 cm)

1 Separate the chain into two 5-link pieces, one 3-link piece, and four 2-link pieces, by opening and closing the links as you would jump rings.

2 Use hole-punch pliers to punch 1 hole in the leaf toggle ring, directly opposite the existing hole. Repeat 3 times, using 2 hammered toggle rings and 1 etched square toggle ring.

3 Place the dragonfly link on top of the leaf toggle ring and use the marker to mark where the 2 holes of the link meet the toggle ring. Use hole-punch pliers to punch the 2 marked holes.

4 Use 1 ball-end head pin to string the top hole of the dragonfly link. Pass through the punched hole in the toggle ring. Bend the head pin to 90° at the back of the toggle ring. Tightly wrap the head pin twice around the toggle ring. Trim the wire end and tuck in the end.

5 Repeat Step 4 using the flower-end head pin, the bottom hole of the dragonfly link, and the remaining punched hole of the leaf toggle ring. Use 2 nylon-jaw pliers or the ring-bending pliers to gently curve the leaf toggle ring so that it mimics the curve around the top of the wrist.

6 Place a thin line of glue around the top edge of 1 aluminum disc. Place the disc beneath 1 hammered toggle ring, making sure 1 hole in the ring is covered by the disc beneath and 1 hole is not. Hold the 2 pieces together for five seconds until the glue bonds. Let dry. Repeat this entire step for a second glued link. On the side of the link with the covered hole, punch a hole through the existing hole in the ring and through the aluminum disc beneath. Repeat with the other glued link.

7 Use 1 ball-end head pin to string the engraved toggle bar, from front to back. Form a double-wrapped loop.

8 Use round-nose pliers to curl both points of 1 leaf toggle bar down under the bar. Repeat with the other leaf toggle bar. Use 2 nylon-jaw pliers or ring-bending pliers to form a gentle curve in both toggle bars.

9 Use 3" (7.6 cm) of wire to string 1 leaf toggle bar. Use about 1" (2.5 cm) of the wire to form a wrapped loop, pulling the wire so that the loop is wrapped tightly around the edge of the toggle bar. Use the other end of the wire to form a wrapped loop. Use 3" (7.6 cm) of wire and repeat with the same toggle bar, on the opposite side of the bar. Repeat this entire step with the second leaf toggle bar.

10 Use 6" (15.2 cm) of wire to string 1 cream-and-brown polymer clay rondelle. Wrap about 2" (5.1 cm) of wire up and around the rondelle and coil it around the wire at the top of the rondelle. Coil the wire several times around itself. Pass the other end of the wire through the center link of one 5-link chain and string 1 cream-and-green polymer clay rondelle. Wrap the wire up and around the rondelle and coil it around the wire between the rondelle and the chain. Coil the wire several times around itself. Repeat this entire step.

11 Use the 3-link chain to attach the engraved toggle bar wrapped loop to the etched square toggle ring with 2 holes.

12 Use one 2-link chain to attach the other hole of the square toggle ring to 1 loop of 1 leaf toggle bar.

13 Use one 2-link chain to attach the other loop of the leaf toggle bar to 1 hammered toggle ring.

14 Use one 5-link chain to attach the other hole of the hammered toggle ring to 1 hole of the leaf toggle ring, making sure the cream-and-brown polymer clay rondelle is on top. Repeat for the other half of the leaf toggle ring, making sure the cream-and-green polymer clay rondelle is on top.

15 Use one 2-link chain to attach the other hole of the hammered toggle ring to 1 loop of the remaining leaf toggle bar.

16 Use one 2-link chain to attach the other loop of the leaf toggle bar to the remaining etched square toggle ring.

Tidal Treasures

A perforated toggle clasp
reminiscent of a sea urchin makes
a perfect multistrand connector
in this luscious, ocean-worthy
necklace full of ivory,
soft greens, and silver.

MOLLY SCHALLER

Materials

- 1 pewter 16×22mm fish bead
- 54 evergreen 4×6mm pressed-glass teardrops
- 37 white top-drilled 6–8mm keishi pearls
- 33 (about 1 gram) matte sea green swirl 2×4mm peanut beads (A)
- 95 (about 3 grams) celadon opal luster 2×4mm peanut beads (B)
- 90 (about 3 grams) asparagus swirl luster 2×4mm peanut beads (C)
- 70 (about ¼ gram) dark gold-lined crystal 15° seed beads (D)
- 28" (71 cm) strand of fine silver faceted 2.5mm cornerless cubes
- 1 pewter 48×16mm coral connector
- 1 sterling silver 16×18mm flattened hollow cone with hammered finish
- 1 silver polka dot ruffle 25mm **toggle clasp**
- 2 silver 6mm jump rings
- 1 silver 8mm jump ring
- 10 silver-plated 2mm crimp tubes
- 36" (91.4 cm) of ¾" (1.9 cm) douppioni silk ribbon
- 12" (30.5 cm) of 20-gauge sterling silver wire
- 77" (2 m) of .018" flexible beading wire

Tools

Round-nose pliers
2 pairs of chain- or flat-nose pliers
Crimping pliers
Wire cutters
Bead stops
Scissors

Techniques *(see page 130)*

Crimping ▪ Jump rings ▪ Lark's head knot ▪ Stringing ▪ Wire wrapping ▪ Wrapped loops

Finished Size

28" (71.1 cm) (shortest length)

1 Cut 12" (30.5 cm) of flexible beading wire. Place the toggle bar horizontally on top of the ruffle/ring half of the clasp. String 1 crimp tube and 5 seed beads (D) and then pass the wire through a hole in the ruffle of the ring clasp at about the 5 o'clock point of the toggle when the bar is horizontal. String 5D, pass the wire back through the tube, and crimp the tube with crimping pliers.

2 String 1D and 1 teardrop; repeat 3 times. String 3 matte sea green swirl peanuts (A).

3 String 1D and 1 teardrop; repeat 4 times. String 3A.

4 Repeat Steps 2 and 3 five more times. String 10D and 1 crimp tube. Attach a bead stop to the end of the wire. This is Strand 1.

TIP
Run the silk ribbon through your hands a few times to create a frayed edge for a romantic touch.

5 Cut 9" (22.9 cm) of flexible beading wire. String 1 crimp tube, 5D, and the next hole in the ruffle/ring clasp to the left of the previous attached wire. String 5D, pass the wire back through the tube and crimp. String 28 pearls, 1 crimp tube, and the hole in one end of the pewter coral connector. Pass the wire back through the tube and crimp.

6 Cut 6" (15.2 cm) of flexible beading wire. String 1 crimp tube and the hole in the other end of the pewter coral connector. Pass the wire back through the tube and crimp. String 9 pearls, 10D, and 1 crimp tube. Add the wire to the bead stop. This is Strand 2.

7 Cut 15" (38.1 cm) of flexible beading wire. String 1 crimp tube, 5D, the next hole in the ruffle/ring clasp to the left of the previous attached wire. String 5D, pass the wire back through the tube and crimp. String 12½" (31.8 cm) of 2.5mm beads and 1 crimp tube. Add the wire to the bead stop. This is Strand 3.

8 Cut 17" (43.2 cm) of flexible beading wire. String 1 crimp tube, 5D, the next hole in the ruffle/ring clasp to the left of the previous attached wire. String 5D, pass the wire back through the tube, and crimp. String 5 celadon opal luster peanuts (B) and 5 asparagus swirl luster peanuts (C); repeat 17 times. String 5B and 1 crimp tube. Add the wire to the bead stop. This is Strand 4.

9 Cut 18" (45.7 cm) of flexible beading wire. String 1 crimp tube, 5D, the next hole in the ruffle/ring clasp to the left of the previous attached wire. String 5D, pass the wire back through the crimp tube and crimp. String 15" of 2.5mm beads and 1 crimp tube. Add the wire to the bead stop. This is Strand 5.

Variation

Use a sun-themed copper-plated toggle clasp with lots of holes to create a bright bracelet such as this one by Michelle Mach. The bracelet features striped green glass leaves, an assortment of glass and wood beads in shades of yellow, brown, and orange, tiny copper seed beads, and leafy copper-plated chain.

10 Cut 4" (10.2 cm) of silver wire. Make a large (about ¼" [6 mm]) wrapped loop on one end.

11 Remove Strand 1 from the bead stop and pass the end of the flexible beading wire through the wrapped loop and back through the crimp tube. Snug the beads and crimp the tube. Repeat this step to attach Strands 2, 3, 4, and 5 in that order, from shortest to longest.

12 Pass the long end of the silver wire through the large end of the cone, pulling the beaded strands inside. Make a wrapped loop and trim the excess wire.

13 Attach one 6mm jump ring to each of the 2 loops on the end of the toggle bar. Attach the 8mm jump ring to both 6mm jump rings. Fold the silk ribbon in half and make a lark's head knot through the 8mm jump ring.

14 Pass the tail ends of the ribbon through the wrapped loop at the top of the cone and fold the ends back on themselves. Begin a small simple loop on one end of the remaining 8" (20.3 cm) piece of silver wire. Insert the doubled over ribbon into the loop and close the loop. Continue wrapping the silver wire 3–5 times around the ribbon to secure it to the cone. Slide the fish bead, tail first, onto the wire, and then wrap the wire around the ribbon above the fish's mouth 3–5 times. Trim the wire and tuck the tail into the ribbon.

Wishing Tree

Hook-and-eye clasps make a pretty chain and a clever bail in this sweet necklace complete with a bird bead perched in a bead-cap nest.

VARIATION

Create matching earrings by using a head pin to string a spacer, an open flower, a jump ring, and a bird bead and then form a wrapped loop. Use 22g craft wire to wrap the flower and jump ring together, creating the look of a nest.

MICHELLE MACH

Materials

- 1 purple/brown/blue 25×42mm porcelain rectangle pendant
- 1 copper 25×27mm tree pendant
- 1 copper-plated 14×10mm bird bead
- 2 copper size 11° metal round seed beads
- 1 purple 9×11mm faceted-glass helix
- 4 apatite 8mm nuggets
- 2 lilac 8×6mm ceramic rondelles
- 4 Montana blue 6×4mm faceted-glass rondelles
- 6 blue 5×3mm fire-polished glass rondelles
- 2 amethyst 6mm faceted rounds
- 1 copper-plated 10×6mm bead cap
- 15 copper-plated 8×23mm **hook-and-eye clasps** (11 hooks, 15 eyes)
- 2 copper-plated 4mm rope spacers
- 8 brass 2" (5.1 cm) eye pins
- 27 brass 4mm jump rings
- 2 copper 10mm jump rings
- 7" (17.8 cm) of bronze 26-gauge craft wire

Tools

Round-nose pliers
2 pairs of chain- or flat-nose pliers
Wire cutters

Techniques *(see page 130)*

Jump rings ■ Simple loops ■ Wire wrapping

Finished Size

18" (45.7 cm)

Tip

For extra security and added decoration, wrap 24 or 26g wire several times around the middle of the closed S-clasp hooks. Tuck in the wire ends to ensure a snag-free jewelry-wearing experience.of a nest. Use a jump ring to attach the wrapped loop to a leverback ear wire.

1 Attach the top of the tree pendant to the loop of 1 hook clasp. Slide the hook/tree pendant over the front of the porcelain pendant with the hook loop just below the hole in the porcelain pendant. Pinch the hook closed with your fingers, being careful not to mar the porcelain. Use 4" (10.2 cm) of craft wire to wrap 3–4 times around the hook, just above the loop. Pass the wire through the pendant from front-to-back and wrap 3–4 times around the other end of the hook.

2 Use 1 eye pin to string 1 rope spacer, 1 purple helix, and 1 rope spacer; form a simple loop. Use 1 eye pin to string 2 apatite nuggets and 1 lilac round; form a simple loop. Repeat. Use 1 eye pin to string 2 Montana blue rondelles; form a simple loop. Repeat. Use 1 eye pin to string 3 blue fire-polished rondelles; form a simple loop. Repeat. Use 1 eye pin to string 1 copper seed bead, the bead cap, the bird, and another copper seed bead; form a simple loop. *Use 1½" (3.8 cm) of craft wire to wrap one side of one 10mm copper jump ring 4 times. String 1 amethyst in the center of the ring and wrap the remaining wire 4 times around the opposite side of the jump ring. Repeat from *.

3 Attach the bottom loop of the purple helix link to the hook on the pendant. Use 1 brass jump ring to attach the top loop to 2 brass jump rings.

4 Attach the left jump ring from Step 3 to the left hole of 1 eye. Attach the large end of 1 hook to this hole. Use flat-nose pliers to pinch the clasp closed so that both ends touch. Use 1 brass jump ring to attach the loop end of the hook to 1 apatite-and-ceramic link. Use brass jump rings to attach the remaining elements in this order: the bird link, the Montana blue link, the amethyst jump ring, and the blue fire-polished rondelles link.

5 Use 1 brass jump ring to attach the previous link to the large end of 1 hook. Pinch the hook closed. Attach the loop end of the hook to 1 hole of 1 eye. Attach the loop end of 1 hook to the other hole of the eye. Use 1 brass jump ring to attach the large end of the previous hook to the loop end of 1 hook. Attach the large end of the previous hook to 1 hole of 1 eye. Pinch both hooks closed.

6 Use 1 brass jump ring to attach the other hole of the previous eye to 1 hole of 1 eye. Repeat 4 times. Attach the loop end of 1 hook to the free hole of the last eye, leaving the hook open.

7 Repeat Steps 4–6 attaching the right jump ring from Step 3 to the other half of the necklace, substituting 1 hook for the bird link and omitting the hook at the end of the chain.

Washer Woman

Copper washers from the hardware store make not only inexpensive link/connectors but rings for a custom toggle clasp.

ERIN STROTHER

Materials

- 1 iolite 20×5.5mm faceted nugget
- 1 crystal quartz 15×4.5mm point
- 1 white 6mm pearl
- 1 iolite 12mm briolette
- 1 vintage 2" (5.1 cm) key
- 1 copper 15mm washer link
- 2 copper 17mm washer links
- 2 copper 14mm washer links
- 9 stainless steel 12mm washer links
- 1 bronze 12mm washer link
- 1 copper 2" (5.1 cm) head pin
- 1 aluminum 9mm jump ring
- 2 copper 9mm jump rings
- 2 copper 6mm jump rings
- 9 antique brass 9mm jump rings
- 2 brass 6mm jump rings
- 3 brass 4mm jump rings
- 1 copper 18mm toggle bar
- 1 stainless steel 9×3mm ball-chain connector
- 1 copper ball 9×3mm chain connector
- 6 links antique brass 4mm cable chain
- 24" (61 cm) of stainless steel 1.8mm ball chain
- 12" (30.5 cm) of copper 1.8mm ball chain
- 23" (58.4 cm) of copper 24-gauge wire

Tools

Round-nose pliers
2 pairs of chain-nose pliers
2 pairs of utility hardware pliers
Wire cutters
Ball-peen hammer
Bench block
Liver of sulfur (optional)
Polishing cloth (optional)

Techniques *(see page 130)*

Double-wrapped loops ■
Hammering ■ Jump rings ■
Stringing ■ Wire wrapping ■ Wrapped
loops ■ Oxidizing (optional)

Finished Size

21½" (54.6 cm)

1 Use the ball end of the ball-peen hammer to add texture to all the washers on the bench block. Use 2 pairs of utility pliers to randomly bend both 14mm copper washers and all the stainless steel washers to create dimension.

2 Cut 10" (25.4 cm) of wire and string the iolite briolette 1" (2.5 cm) from one end. Bend both ends of the wire up the sides of the briolette and form a double-loop briolette wrapped loop, wrapping down the tip of the briolette and back up again. Trim the wires and tuck in the end. Open 1 link on the end of the cable chain and attach it to the briolette loop; close the link. Attach the free end of the chain to 1 brass 9mm jump ring. Set aside.

3 Cut 10" (25.4 cm) of wire and string the crystal point 1" (2.5 cm) from the end of the wire. Bend both ends of the wire up the sides of the crystal and form a double-loop briolette wrapped loop. Use 1 head pin to string 1 pearl; form a wrapped loop. Use 1 brass 4mm jump ring to attach the loop on the crystal and pearl to 1 brass 9mm jump ring. Set aside.

4 Attach the stainless steel ball chain connector to each end of the stainless ball chain. Attach 1 brass 6mm jump ring to the chain. Use 1 brass 4mm jump ring to attach the previous jump ring to the toggle bar.

5 Use 2 brass 9mm jump rings to attach the stainless steel chain to the bronze washer. Use 2 brass 9mm jump rings to attach the bronze washer to 1 copper 17mm washer and 1 stainless washer, so the stainless washer lies on top of the copper washer.

6 String the copper ball chain through the copper and steel washer from Step 5, so both ends are the same length. Use both ends of the chain to string 1 steel washer, 1 aluminum jump ring, 1 brass 9mm jump ring, the jump ring with the iolite/chain dangle, 1 steel washer, 1 copper 14mm washer, and 1 brass 9mm jump ring. Use one 4mm brass jump ring to attach the 9mm jump ring to 1 brass 6mm jump ring. Attach the 6mm jump ring to the key. String 2 steel washers, 1 copper 14mm washer, the 9mm ring with the crystal and pearl dangles, 1 aluminum jump ring, and 3 steel washers.

7 String one end of the chain through 1 copper 17mm washer and attach both ends of the chain together with the copper ball-chain connector.

8 Cut 3" (7.6 cm) of wire and form a double-loop wrapped loop on one end. String the iolite nugget and form a double-loop wrapped loop. Use 1 copper 6mm jump ring to attach 1 wrapped loop to the copper washer from Step 7. Use 1 copper 6mm jump ring to attach the other wrapped loop to a steel washer. Use 2 copper 9mm rings to attach the steel washer to 1 copper 15mm washer.

9 Oxidize the necklace using liver of sulfur solution to darken the copper and brass. Rinse and dry. Use a polishing cloth to bring up some shiny highlights.

Midnight Waltz

Fine chain adds movement to these elegant earrings made with flattened bead caps, making them especially fun to wear while dancing.

VARIATION
Use the tip of your round-nose pliers to curl the petals of tiny copper bead caps. A wrapped loop hidden at the back of the earrings keeps the pewter spacer centered on the front of these dainty purple crystal pearl earrings.

MICHELLE MACH

Materials

- 4 matte copper 3×4mm fire-polished glass rounds
- 2 navy 8×14mm faceted-glass ovals
- 2 copper 8×13mm filigree bead caps
- 2 brass 2" (5.1 cm) eye pins
- 4 copper 4mm jump rings
- 6 copper 6mm jump rings
- 2 brass ear wires
- 7" (17.8 cm) of brass 1.5mm cable chain
- 13" (33 cm) of copper 2mm cable chain

Tools

Round-nose pliers
2 pairs of chain- or flat-nose pliers
Wire cutters

Techniques *(see page 130)*

Filigree forming ▪ Jump rings ▪ Simple loops

Finished Size

4½" (11.4 cm)

1 Cut the copper chain into two 4¼" (10.8 cm) pieces and two 2¼" (5.7 cm) pieces. Cut the brass chain into two 3½" (8.9 cm) pieces.

2 Use flat-nose pliers to bend one side of the bead cap outward to form a 90° angle. Repeat twice for the other 2 sides of the bead cap.

3 Use 1 eye pin to string 1 copper round, 1 navy oval, and 1 copper round; form a simple loop. Attach the top loop to 1 ear wire. Use one 6mm copper jump ring to attach the bottom loop to one side of the bead cap.

4 Attach one 6mm jump ring to the left bottom side of the bead cap. Use one 4mm jump ring to attach the previous 6mm jump ring to one end of one 4¼" (10.8 cm) copper chain, one 3½" (8.9 cm) brass chain, and one 2¼" (5.7 cm) copper chain. Repeat this entire step, attaching the other ends of all 3 chains to the right side of the bead cap.

5 Repeat Steps 2–4 for the second earring.

Variation

See Brazen Blooms by Denise Yezbak Moore (page 68) for another idea using flattened bead caps.

Tips

Thin filigree bead caps and cones are the easiest to flatten, but be aware that if you bend them back and forth several times, they may break.

Save all your short snippets of chain left over from your bracelet and necklace projects to make earrings.

Rings Around the Monarch

Chartreuse, orange, and brass jump-ring rosettes provide a gardenlike setting for a stunning handmade glass butterfly. The two swirl hook clasps in the front may be connected sans pendant for a simpler look.

TIP

In making jump-ring rosettes, always move the rings in the same direction so that they lie flat.

Materials

- 1 green-and-red 26mm lampwork-glass focal butterfly
- 25 carnelian AB top-drilled faceted onion briolettes
- 170 (about 2 grams) frosted green size 11° seed beads
- 7 chartreuse green 10mm anodized aluminum jump rings
- 7 orange 10mm anodized aluminum jump rings
- 39 etched brass 9mm jump rings
- 5 copper 10mm jump rings
- 2 brass 10mm jump rings
- 13 copper 2mm crimp tubes
- 8 brass 3mm crimp covers
- 2 brass swirl 16×11mm hook clasps
- 1 chartreuse 18" (45.7 cm) silk 6mm flat cord
- 7" (17.8 cm) of vintage bronze 20-gauge craft wire
- 22" (55.9 cm) of .018" flexible beading wire

Tools

2 pairs of chain- or flat-nose pliers
Crimping pliers
Wire cutters
4 bead stops (optional)

Techniques *(see page 130)*

Chain maille ■ Crimp covers ■ Crimping ■ Double-loop wrapped loops ■ Jump rings ■ Stringing ■ Wire wrapping

Finished Size

18" (45.7 cm)

ERIN PRAIS-HINTZ

1 Use 2 pairs of chain- or flat-nose pliers to open all the jump rings.

2 Use 1 chartreuse jump ring to pick up 1 orange jump ring; close both rings. Place the rings on top of each other and then use 1 etched brass jump ring to pick up the 2 joined rings, forming 1 chain-maille rosette. Repeat this entire step for a total of 7 rosettes.

3 Use 1 etched jump ring to pick up 1 rosette from Step 1; close the ring. Attach 1 more etched jump ring to the other side of the same rosette; close the ring. Repeat with the remaining 6 rosettes, forming a total of 7 rosette links.

4 Cut the flexible beading wire into the following pieces: four 3" (7.6 cm) pieces and five 2" (5.1 cm) pieces.

5 Use one 3" (7.6 cm) piece of flexible beading wire to string 1 etched ring on 1 rosette link and 1 crimp tube. Pass the flexible beading wire back through the tube and crimp the tube using crimping pliers. Cover the tube with a crimp cover. String 5 briolettes, 1 crimp tube, and 1 etched jump ring on another rosette link. Pass the flexible beading wire back through the tube and crimp. Cover the tube with a crimp cover. Repeat this entire step, attaching the second 3" (7.6 cm) flexible beading wire to the previous etched jump ring. Set aside.

6 Repeat Step 5 for the other side of the necklace. Attach 1 brass swirl hook to 1 etched jump ring on the end of each strand.

7 Create 4 rosettes using 3 etched jump rings each.

8 String the silk cord through the free etched jump ring on the end of 1 strand. Center the etched jump ring on the cord.

9 String all 4 rosettes from Step 7 onto the cord. Push 2 rosettes down to the etched jump ring attached to the strand.

10 Cut 2" (5.1 cm) of craft wire. String both tail ends of the cord through 1 etched jump ring on one end of the second strand and fold the ends around the etched jump ring. Wrap the cord ends with craft wire tightly to secure. Push the 2 free rosettes over the wrapped wire to hide it.

11 Use the remaining 5" (12.7 cm) of craft wire and create a double-loop wrapped loop at one end. String the focal butterfly and make a second double-loop wrapped loop.

12 String 1 etched jump ring through the top loop on the focal bead and the center of the rosette on the remaining rosette link from Step 3. Attach one 10mm brass jump rings to the etched rings of the rosette link.

13 Connect 5 etched brass jump rings in a chain, attaching 1 jump ring to the bottom loop of the focal bead.

14 Use 2" (5.1 cm) of flexible beading wire to string 1 crimp tube, 10 seed beads, 1 briolette, and 10 seed beads. Pass the tail of the flexible beading wire through the crimp tube, forming a circle. Carefully crimp the tube with crimping pliers. (**Tip:** Place the tip of your fingernail over the closest seed bead to the crimp so that the pressure of crimping doesn't crack the glass seed bead.) Trim the wires. Repeat this entire step 4 times for a total of 5 beaded dangles.

15 Use one 10mm jump ring to string 14 seed beads. Repeat 4 times to create a total of 5 beaded jump rings. Attach 1 beaded dangle and 1 beaded jump ring to each link of the etched jump ring chain attached to the bottom of the focal.

16 Connect each 10mm brass jump ring on the focal butterfly to the swirl clasps on the necklace strands.

Brazen Blooms

Create bold flowers reminiscent of Georgia O'Keeffe with layers of flattened bead caps. Add bright orange ribbon and metallic blue glass beads to complete this Bohemian-style necklace.

DENISE YEZBAK MOORE

Materials

- 11 blue iris 5×7mm faceted-glass rondelles
- 6 orange AB 5×6mm faceted-glass cubes
- 7 brass 22×14mm flourish petal bead caps
- 3 brass 12mm filigree bead caps
- 3 brass 7.5mm ornate bead caps
- 3 brass 7mm filigree bead caps
- 11 brass 2" (5.1 cm) eye pins
- 3 brass 2" (5.1 cm) head pins
- 2 brass 4mm jump rings
- 1 brass 24×11mm hook
- 24" (61 cm) of orange sari silk
- 7" (17.8 cm) of 6.5×9.5mm etched unsoldered brass cable chain (20 links)
- Superglue

Tools

Round-nose pliers
2 pairs of chain- or flat-nose pliers
Wire cutters
1.8mm metal hole-punch pliers
Scissors

Techniques *(see page 130)*

Filigree forming ▪ Gluing ▪ Hole punching ▪ Jump rings ▪ Overhand knots ▪ Simple loops

Finished Size

20½" (52.1 cm)

Variation

Replace the fraying sari silk with smooth leather cord for a sleeker look.

1. Open 6 of the flourish beads caps until they are flat. Repeat for the 12mm filigree bead caps and the 7.5mm ornate bead caps.

2. Trim the length of 1 head pin to 1½" (3.8 cm). String 1 blue iris rondelle, 2 opened flourish bead caps (stacked with all 6 petals showing), 1 opened 12mm filigree bead cap, 1 opened 7.5mm bead cap, one 7mm bead cap, and 1 blue iris rondelle. Using round-nose pliers, coil the head pin down until it fits snugly against the bead. Repeat this entire step 2 times ending with an orange cube on top instead of a blue iris rondelle.

3. Using the hole-punch pliers, punch a hole on the left and right side of the top flourish bead cap on the blue iris set. Repeat on the 2 orange sets. Set aside.

4. Use 1 eye pin to string 1 blue iris rondelle. Trim the wire and form a simple loop. Repeat 5 times. Use 1 eye pin to string 1 orange cube. Trim the wire and form a simple loop. Repeat 3 times.

5. Remove 17 links from the chain, opening and closing the links as you would jump rings. Set 1 link aside for clasp. Connect the necklace in the following order: 2 links, orange cube loop, 2 links, blue iris loop, 2 links, orange cube loop, 2 links, blue iris loop, jump ring, orange flourish set, blue iris loop, blue iris flourish set, blue iris loop, orange flourish set, jump ring, blue iris loop, 2 links, orange cube loop, 2 links, blue iris loop, 2 links, orange cube loop, and 2 links.

6. Use 1 eye pin to string 1 blue iris rondelle and the remaining flourish bead cap; form a simple loop. Connect 1 link of chain to the eye-pin loop on top of the bead cap. Connect 3 links of chain to the simple loop inside the bead cap. Attach the hook to the end of the 3-link chain. Set aside.

7. Cut the sari silk into two 12" (30.5 cm) lengths. String 1 piece through the 2 end links on the left side of the necklace and form an overhand knot. Measure 2½" (6.4 cm) from the previous knot and make a second overhand knot. Trim the tails and dab the knot with glue to secure. Let dry.

8. String the remaining piece of silk through the 2 end links on the right side of the necklace and form an overhand knot. Measure 2½" (6.4 cm) from the previous knot and string the chain link on top of the bead cap clasp. Form an overhand knot, trim the tails, and dab the knot with glue to secure. Let dry.

"I find inspiring color combinations from magazine layouts, photos of nature, paint swatches, and fabrics. Try keeping a scrapbook of all your favorite color combinations."—Denise Yezbak Moore

Zero Hour

Layers of copper, brass, and silver jump rings form a timeless pendant that is easy to wear and perfect for any event, whether it's an important meeting at work or a secret spy mission.

TIP

This project uses only the bar half of a toggle clasp. Use the leftover toggle ring to make a simple pendant inspired by Erin's Ancient Artifacts earrings (page 84).

ERIN STROTHER

Materials

- 2 copper 4mm fluted rounds
- 1 copper 6mm fluted round
- 1 copper 17mm washer
- 1 copper 20mm washer
- 13 copper 4mm jump rings
- 2 copper 6mm jump rings
- 5 copper 9mm jump rings
- 6 brass 3mm jump rings
- 9 brass 4mm jump rings
- 13 brass 6mm jump rings
- 28 brass 9mm jump rings
- 1 brass 12mm jump ring
- 2 brass 12mm jump rings, blackened
- 4 silver 6mm jump rings
- 1 silver 9mm jump ring
- 1 brass 26.5mm toggle bar
- 12" (30.5 cm) of brass 24-gauge wire
- 2" (5.1 cm) of brass 16-gauge wire
- 10" (25.4 cm) of brown ³/₁₆" (4.8 mm) leather lace

Tools

2 pairs chain-nose pliers
Round-nose pliers
Wire cutters
Ball-peen hammer
Bench block
Liver of sulfur (optional)

Techniques *(see page 130)*

Hammering ▪ Jump rings ▪ Lark's head knot ▪ Simple loops ▪ Texturizing ▪ Wire wrapping ▪ Oxidizing (optional)

Finished Size

16" (40.6 cm)

Note: All of the jump rings will be referred to as "rings" in the instructions below.

1 If desired, oxidize all the findings except the already blackened brass 12mm rings in a liver of sulfur solution. Rinse and dry. Use the ball end of the ball-peen hammer to add texture to both copper washers on the bench block.

2 Close 4 copper 4mm rings and 5 brass 4mm rings; set aside.

3 Use 2 copper 9mm rings to attach 1 copper 20mm washer to 1 blackened brass 12mm ring.

4 Attach 2 silver 6mm rings to the washer on each side of the copper rings. Use 1 blackened brass 12mm ring to string all 6 rings attached to the washer so it sits on top of the washer. Before closing the blackened ring, attach all 9 rings from Step 2; close the ring. Weave 1 copper 9mm ring through the same path so it sits inside the blackened 12mm ring; close the ring.

5 Close 4 copper 4mm rings and 4 brass 4mm rings; set aside.

6 Flatten one end of the 16g wire into a paddle using the hammer and bench block. String 1 copper 4mm fluted round, 2 brass 3mm rings, 3 copper 4mm rings, 1 brass 3mm ring, 1 copper 6mm fluted round, 1 brass 3mm ring, 2 copper 4mm rings, 1 brass 3mm ring, 1 copper 4mm fluted round, and 1 brass 3mm ring. Form a simple loop.

7 Use 1 copper 6mm ring to attach 1 brass 12mm ring, 1 silver 9mm ring, and 1 copper 6mm ring to the bottom of the copper washer, forming concentric circles. Open the brass 12mm ring and string 2 brass 4mm rings and 2 copper 4mm rings (from Step 5), the dangle (from Step 6), 2 more copper 4mm rings, and 2 more brass 4mm rings (from Step 5). Close the 12mm ring to complete the pendant.

8 Fold the leather lace in half and use a lark's head knot to attach it to the blackened 12mm ring at the top of the pendant. Slide 5 brass 6mm rings onto each leather strip.

9 Fold 1 leather tail over 1 copper 9mm ring so it overlaps about ¾" (1.9 cm). Cut 6" (15.2 cm) of 24g wire and wrap it tightly around the leather end, overlapping the wraps to secure. Tuck the wire tails into the wraps. Repeat this entire step for the other leather strip.

10 Connect 14 brass 9mm rings together to form a simple chain. Attach one end of the chain to the copper ring from Step 9. Use 2 brass 6mm rings to attach the other end of the chain to the toggle bar.

11 Repeat Step 10 for the other side of the necklace using 1 brass 6mm ring to attach the copper 17mm washer to the end of the chain.

Secrets of Jade

By doubling delicate filigree connectors for strength and adding simple beaded links for structure, you can create a luscious and durable bracelet.

TIP

The center cluster element in Step 10 is made from a large number of wire-wrapped dangles. Because the cluster will need to be tight, it is easiest to wrap the dangles directly onto the front of the jump ring.

BARB SWITZER

Materials

- 22 blue zircon 2×3mm faceted-crystal rondelles
- 4 emerald 8mm crystal rounds
- 12 blue zircon 4mm crystal rounds
- 6 jade-colored 5mm crystal pearls
- 24 silver 4mm daisy spacers
- 26–30 silver 3mm daisy spacers
- 4 silver 15×18mm 1-to-3 filigree connectors
- 26–30 silver 1½" (3.8 cm) 26-gauge head pins
- 3 silver 16-gauge 8mm jump rings
- 4 silver 18-gauge 5mm jump rings
- 1 silver 12×18.5mm filigree box clasp
- 5" (12.7 cm) of silver 18-gauge wire
- 6" (15.2 cm) of silver 20-gauge wire

Tools

Round-nose pliers
2 pairs of chain- or flat-nose pliers
Wire cutters

Techniques *(see page 130)*

Jump rings ■ Simple loops ■ Wire wrapping

Finished Size

6½" (16.5 cm)

Instead of using filigree connectors throughout the bracelet, Molly Schaller used chandelier earring findings just at the ends. Her choice of soft, ocean-inspired beads evokes a completely different mood than the original.

1 Cut 1¼" (3.2 cm) of 18g wire and form a simple loop on one end of the wire using round-nose pliers. String one 4mm daisy spacer, one 8mm crystal round, and one 4mm daisy spacer. Trim the wire and form a second simple loop. Repeat this entire step 3 times for a total of 4 A-links (4A).

2 Cut ¾" (1.9 cm) of 20g wire and form a simple loop on one end of the wire. String one 4mm daisy spacer, 1 crystal rondelle, and one 4mm daisy spacer. Trim the wire and form a second simple loop. Repeat this entire step 7 times for a total of 8 B-links (8B).

3 Place 2 filigree connectors back-to-back, forming a set. Attach 1 loop of 1A to the center holes on the 3-strand end of the connector set; close the loop. Attach the other loop on 1A to the corresponding center holes on a second connector set. Set aside.

4 Repeat Step 3.

5 Use one 5mm jump ring to connect 2B together. Repeat, with the remaining B-links for a total of 4 sets.

6 Attach 1 set from Step 5 to the outer holes on the 3-strand end of the connector sets in Step 3. Repeat to connect the outer holes on the other side. Repeat this entire step to connect the other connector sets from Step 4.

7 Use one 16g jump ring to connect 2 single-strand ends together at the center of the bracelet; close the jump ring.

8 Attach 1 loop of 1A to the remaining connector hole on one end of the bracelet. Use one 16mm jump ring to connect one half of the clasp to the other loop on the link. Repeat this entire step for the other end of the bracelet.

9 Use 1 head pin to string 1 pearl and one 3mm daisy spacer. Form the loop portion of a wrapped loop but do not wrap it. Set aside. Repeat for the remaining pearls.

10 Use the remaining head pins to create dangles in various sizes, stacking 1 or 2 crystals plus a 3mm daisy spacer onto each head pin. Form the loop above the bead stack as in Step 9. Connect 1 loop at a time to the front of the center jump ring, complete the wrap, and trim the wire. Attach 3 small and then 1 large dangle until they cluster tightly together when the bracelet is flat or on your wrist. (Fold the bracelet halves together, pulling them toward the back, to make extra room on the jump ring for the dangles.)

Enchanted Forest

Turn crimp cord ends into links in this shimmering copper-and-earth-tone necklace with two different detachable pendants: a pale green ceramic tree pendant and a shimmering metallic charmed pendant.

TIP

Before crimping the second crimp of any of the strung sections, make sure that the wire isn't twisted so that all the leaf ends face right side up.

JAMIE HOGSETT

Materials for beaded strand

- 1 blue/white/black/green/yellow/gray/brown 21×16mm spotted lampwork-glass rondelle
- 2 white with green dots 9×7mm lampwork-glass rondelles
- 5 bronze-and-brown 11×7mm polymer clay rondelles
- 5 white/blue/brown/black 14–15mm polymer clay rounds
- 4 powder green 12mm crystal pearls
- 4 Tahitian 12mm crystal pearls
- 4 copper 12mm crystal pearls
- 51 dark aqua azure luster size 11° seed beads (A)
- 25 hematite matte 2×4mm peanut seed beads (B)
- 1 brass leaf 1mm leather cord crimp-end hook-and-eye clasp set
- 2 copper leaf 1mm leather cord crimp-end eyes
- 2 silver leaf 1mm leather cord crimp-end eye
- 1 brass leaf 1mm leather cord crimp-end eye
- 3 brass 2" (5 cm) head pins
- 2 copper 2" (5 cm) head pins
- 2 silver 2" (5 cm) head pins
- 12 copper 2mm crimp tubes
- 4 brass 3mm crimp covers
- 4 copper 3mm crimp covers
- 4 silver 3mm crimp covers
- 36" (91.5 cm) of dark blue lapis .019 flexible beading wire

Tools

Round-nose pliers
2 pairs of chain- or flat-nose pliers
Nylon-jaw pliers
Crimping pliers
Wire cutters

Techniques *(see page 130)*

Crimping ■ Crimp covers ■ Jump rings
Stringing ■ Wrapped loops

Finished Size

23" (58.4 cm)

BEADED STRAND

1 Use 1 brass head pin to string 1 brass leaf crimp-end eye with the pin exiting toward the tip of the leaf; string 1 size 11° seed bead (A), 1 peanut bead (B), 1 polymer clay round, 1B, and 1A; form a wrapped loop.

2 Repeat Step 1 twice using 2 silver head pins and 2 silver leaf crimp-end eyes. Repeat again using 1 copper head pin and 1 copper leaf crimp-end eye.

3 Use 1 copper head pin to string 1 copper leaf crimp-end eye, 1A, 1B, the lampwork-glass round, 1B, and 1A; form a wrapped loop.

4 Use 1 brass head pin to string 1 brass leaf crimp-end eye with the pin exiting toward the tip of the leaf, 1A, 1B, 1A, 1 polymer clay rondelle, 1A, 1B, and 1A; form a wrapped loop.

5 Use 1 brass head pin to string the crimp-end hook with the pin exiting the crimp-end, 1A, 1B, 1A, 1 polymer clay rondelle, 1A, 1B, and 1A; form a wrapped loop.

6 Use 6" (15 cm) of beading wire to string 1 crimp tube and the eye of the first brass leaf link formed in Step 1. Pass the wire back through the tube and crimp the tube with crimping pliers. Cover the tube using 1 brass crimp cover. String 1A, 1 powder green pearl, 1A, 1B, 1A, 1 polymer clay rondelle, 1A, 1B, 1A, 1 Tahitian pearl, 1A, 1 crimp tube, and the wrapped loop of 1 silver leaf link formed in Step 2. Pass the wire back through the tube, crimp, and cover the tube with 1 brass crimp cover.

7 Use 6" (15.2 cm) of flexible beading wire to string 1 crimp tube and the eye of the previous link. Pass the wire back through the tube, crimp and cover the tube using 1 silver crimp cover. String 1A, 1 copper pearl, 1A, 1B, 1A, 1 polymer clay rondelle, 1A, 1B, 1A, 1 powder green pearl, 1A, 1 crimp tube, and the wrapped loop of the lampwork-bead link. Pass the wire back through the tube, crimp, and cover the tube using 1 copper crimp cover.

8 Use 7" (17.8 cm) of beading wire to string 1 crimp tube and eye of the previous link. Pass the wire back through the tube, crimp and cover the tube using 1 copper crimp cover. String 1A, 1 Tahitian pearl, 1A, 1 copper pearl, 1A, 1B, 1 polymer clay round, 1B, 1A, 1 powder green pearl, 1A, 1 crimp tube, and the eye of the brass leaf link formed in Step 4. Pass the wire back through the tube, crimp, and cover the tube using 1 brass crimp cover.

Variation

Instead of using mostly the eye halves of the clasps, alternate eye and hook halves for a necklace that can be endlessly rearranged.

9 Use 6" (15.2 cm) of beading wire to string 1 crimp tube and the wrapped loop of the previous link. Pass back through the tube, crimp, and cover the tube using 1 brass crimp cover. String 1A, 1 lampwork-glass rondelle, 1A, 1B, 1A, 1 Tahitian pearl, 1A, 1B, 1A, 1 lampwork-glass rondelle, 1A, 1 crimp tube, and the wrapped loop of 1 silver leaf link formed in Step 2. Pass the wire back through the tube, crimp, and cover the tube using 1 silver crimp cover.

10 Use 6" (15.2 cm) of flexible beading wire to string 1 crimp tube and the eye of the previous link. Pass back through the tube, crimp, and cover the tube with 1 silver crimp cover. String 1A, 1 copper pearl, 1A, 1B, 1A, 1 polymer clay rondelle, 1A, 1B, 1A, 1 powder green pearl, 1A, 1 crimp tube, and the wrapped loop of the copper leaf link formed in Step 2. Pass the wire back through the tube, crimp, and cover the tube using 1 copper crimp cover.

11 Use 5" (12.7 cm) of flexible beading wire to string 1 crimp tube and the eye of the previous link. Pass the wire back through the tube, crimp, and cover the tube with 1 copper crimp cover. String 1A, 1 Tahitian pearl, 1A, 1B, 1A, 1 copper pearl, 1A, 1 crimp tube, and the wrapped loop of the brass hook link formed in Step 5. Pass the wire back through the tube, crimp, and cover the tube using 1 brass crimp cover.

Materials for charmed pendant

- 1 beige with brown stamped letters 9×64mm polymer clay pendant
- 1 shimmering rust 12×24mm polymer clay leaf charm
- 1 shimmering green 16×36mm polymer clay leaf charm
- 1 pewter 10×22mm oak leaf charm
- 2 dark aqua-azure luster size 11° seed beads (A)
- 2 hematite matte 2×4mm peanut seed beads (B)
- 1 silver 1mm leather cord crimp-end hook
- 1 silver 2" (5 cm) head pin
- 1 silver 4mm jump ring
- 1 silver 6mm jump ring
- 1 silver 8mm jump ring
- ⅞" (2.2 cm) of silver-plated 3.5×6mm oval/3.5mm round-link etched chain

Materials for tree pendant

- 1 sage green 28×26mm porcelain pendant
- 2 dark aqua-azure luster size 11° seed beads (A)
- 1 hematite matte 2×4 mm peanut seed bead (B)
- 1 copper 1mm leather cord crimp-end hook
- 1 copper 2" (5 cm) head pin

CHARMED PENDANT

Attach the 4mm jump ring to the pewter oak leaf. Use the 8mm jump ring to attach the 4mm jump ring and the green polymer clay charm to one end of the chain. Use the 6mm jump ring to attach the rust polymer clay charm and 1B to the chain, 2 links above the previous jump ring. Use 1 silver head pin to string the silver crimp-end hook, 1A, 1B, and 1A; form a wrapped loop that attaches to the open chain end and the polymer clay pendant.

TREE PENDANT

Use 1 copper head pin to string the copper crimp-end hook, 1A, 1B, and 1A; form a wrapped loop that attaches to the hole in the tree pendant.

Tuesday Night Book Club

Fashion your own book by repurposing a flat cord end normally used for leather bracelets as the book covers.

TIP

Pull the knotting cord through until you have the amount you need and trim so that you still have the needle attached for future projects.

MICHELLE MACH

Materials

- 1 brass 8×18mm key charm
- 1 brass 4.5×20mm rectangle "inspire" charm
- 1 brass 16×20mm diamond filigree connector
- 1 brass 11×6mm filigree tube
- 1 brass 32×5mm 2mm leather cord crimp-end hook-and-eye clasp
- 1 purple-and-gold 20×25mm enamel flat cord end
- 2 brass 4.5mm jump rings
- 2 copper 4mm jump rings
- 15" (38.1 cm) of purple 2mm metallic leather round cord
- 16" (40.6 cm) of beige size 8 silk knotting cord with attached needle
- 8" (20.3 cm) of beige size 1 silk knotting cord with attached needle
- 2" (5.1 cm) of bronze 26-gauge craft wire (optional)
- 3" (2.5 cm) of bronze 22-gauge craft wire
- 1 ivory 8×4" (20.3×10.1 cm) card stock

Tools

Round-nose pliers
2 pairs of chain- or flat-nose pliers
1.8 mm metal hole-punch pliers
Wire cutters
Scissors
Ruler

Techniques (see page 130)

Filigree forming ■ Hole punching ■ Jump rings ■ Overhand knots ■ Wire wrapping (optional)

Finished Size

16" (40.6 cm)

Tip

Unlike a real book, opening and closing this one will wear and eventually break the metal.

1 Punch 1 hole at the bottom of the "inspire" charm. Set aside.

2 Cut the card stock into 1½" x ¾" (3.8×1.9 cm) rectangles. Fold each one in half and stack. Insert the pages into the enamel cord end and gently bend the cord end tight around the pages. Insert the 2" (5.1 cm) 22g craft wire in the middle of the folded pages and form a small loop on each end.

3 Bend the filigree connector around the back of the enamel cord end. Place the "inspire" charm on top of the filigree. Use 1 brass 4.5mm jump ring to attach the bottom wire loop to the bottom hole of the charm and the bottom hole of the filigree. Use 1 copper 4mm jump ring to attach the top hole of the charm and top hole of the filigree. Use 1 copper 4mm jump ring to attach the previous jump ring to the top wire loop. Use 1 brass 4.5mm jump ring to attach the top wire loop to the center of the filigree tube.

4 Use the size 1 silk cord to string the middle ends of the filigree on the front. Repeat for the back. Use both cords to form an overhand knot. Repeat, using the size 8 silk cord, reserving at least 2" (5.1 cm). If necessary, wrap the 26g craft wire around the knot to secure. Use the remaining size 8 silk cord to tie an overhand knot over the wire. Weave the key charm through at least 2 different cords on the front to secure.

5 String half of the leather cord crimp-end clasp on 1 end of the leather cord. Use chain-nose pliers to crimp the prongs of the clasp over the cord to secure. String the book pendant and attach the other half of the crimp-end clasp to the end of the leather cord.

Variation

Can't find a leather cord end exactly like this one? You can easily make your own with a small rectangle of soft metal (22 or 24g). Mark the middle of the rectangle's long edge with a permanent marker. Use your flat-nose pliers to grasp the metal centered over the mark and bend each side up to form the book covers. If desired, punch holes in the spine or the covers to add jump rings or embellishments.

Connect the Dots

Use eye pins to form triangular links
in this charming lattice-style necklace.

TIP

You can often get
more than one link out
of a 2" (5.1 cm) eye pin
when using smaller beads.
It's possible to use only
29 eye pins (instead of 37)
for this necklace by making
two small eye pins from
each eye pin in the
small red links.

MOLLY SCHALLER

Materials

- 15 turquoise/brown Picasso-finish 8×18mm 5-sided tubes
- 2 red 12mm ceramic cantaloupe rounds
- 20 opaque red 8mm faceted-glass rounds
- 8 hammered brass 10mm bead caps
- 37 brass 2" (5.1 cm) **eye pins**
- 12 brass 6mm jump rings
- 8 etched brass 9.5mm jump rings
- 1 brass 8×15mm lobster clasp
- 1¾" (4.4 cm) of etched brass 6.5×9.5mm oval chain (6 links)

Tools

Round-nose pliers
2 pairs of chain-nose pliers
Wire cutters

Finished Size

17¼–18½" (43.8–47 cm) adjustable

Techniques *(see page 130)*

Jump rings ▪ Simple loops ▪ Spirals

"One of my favorite magazines is National Geographic. When I see a photo that resonates with me, I pin it to my inspiration board and pull beads to match."
—Molly Schaller

1 Use 1 eye pin to string 1 red 8mm round. Trim the wire and make a simple loop. Repeat 15 times for a total of 16 red links.

2 Use 1 eye pin to string 1 turquoise/brown glass tube. Trim the wire and make a simple loop. Repeat 14 more times for a total of 15 turquoise links.

3 Use 1 eye pin to string 1 bead cap and 1 red 8mm round. Using chain- or flat-nose pliers, make a 90° bend in the wire at the bottom of the bead. Use round-nose pliers to make a tiny simple loop on the tail of the eye pin. Continue coiling the wire around the loop, forming a spiral. Spiral the wire up to the bead, securing the bead in place. Repeat this entire step 3 times for a total of 4 red spiral dangles.

4 Use 1 eye pin to string 1 bead cap, 1 cantaloupe round, and 1 bead cap. Make a 90° bend in the wire at the bottom of the second bead cap. Spiral the wire as in Step 3, securing the bead in place. Repeat this entire step for a total of 2 cantaloupe spiral dangles.

5 Use two 6mm jump rings to connect 3 turquoise/brown tube links together in a chain. Bring the 2 end links down into a point, creating a triangle shape. Use one 6mm jump ring to connect the link ends of the point together. Connect 2 links to the 6mm jump ring on the right of the triangle. Continue the pattern, connecting all the tube links, and forming a total of 5 triangles.

6 Open the 6mm jump ring attached to the point of the center triangle and attach 1 cantaloupe spiral dangle; close the ring. Attach 1 red spiral dangle to each point on the remaining 4 triangles.

7 Attach 1 red link to the 6mm jump ring on the left corner of the left triangle.

8 Attach 1 etched jump ring to the previous red link. Attach 1 red link to the previous jump ring. Attach 1 red link to the previous red link.

9 Repeat Step 8 two more times. Attach 1 etched jump ring to the previous link. Attach 1 red link to the previous jump ring. Attach the 6-link chain to the previous red link. End this side by attaching 1 cantaloupe spiral dangle to the end of the chain.

10 Repeat Steps 7–9 beginning with the right corner of the right triangle and instead of adding chain, end with one 6mm jump ring and the lobster clasp.

Vertebracelet

Turn three-hole spacer bars sideways and lock them together to form a substantial, slinky cuff with a whole lot of sparkle.

TIP

You'll need half-hard wire for this bracelet. If you only have dead-soft wire, cut a substantial length. Grasp one end in your chain-nose pliers held in your nondominant hand. Grasp the wire with a pair of nylon-jaw pliers and pull the wire through the pliers to the far end. Repeat two or three times, until the wire is springy.

BARB SWITZER

Materials

- 40 lime 3×5mm faceted-crystal rondelles
- 18 khaki 6mm crystal bicones
- 20 jonquil satin 4mm crystal bicones
- 38 khaki 3mm crystal bicones
- 87 (about 2 grams) matte mustard green size 11° seed beads
- 72 silver 4mm daisy spacers
- 38 silver 3mm daisy spacers
- 38 silver 14×6mm 3-hole daisy spacer bars
- 4 sterling silver 6mm 18-gauge jump rings
- 1 sterling silver 2-strand 7×15mm tube bar clasp
- 3' (91.4 cm) of 20-gauge half-hard silver-filled wire
- 3' (91.4 cm) of 22-gauge half-hard silver-filled wire

Tools

Round-nose pliers
2 pairs of chain- or flat-nose pliers
Flush cutters
Nylon-jaw pliers (optional)

Techniques *(see page 130)*

Jump rings ▪ Pinched-end head pins ▪ Stringing

Finished Size

6¾" (17.1 cm)

"Art is subjective: it is key that you love what you make and enjoy the process."
—Barb Switzer

Note: *You will be working from the full length of 20g and 22g wires to prevent waste.*

1 Flush-cut one end of the 20g wire.

2 Use the cut end to string 1 seed bead, one 4mm daisy spacer, the end hole of 1 spacer bar, 1 rondelle, the end hole of 1 spacer bar, one 6mm bicone, the end hole of 1 spacer bar, 1 rondelle, the end hole of 1 spacer bar, one 4mm daisy spacer, and 1 seed bead.

3 Use chain-nose pliers to bend about ¹⁄₁₆" (1.6mm) on the cut end of the wire into a hairpin bend. Pinch the bend closed and center the bent end over the long wire. Trim the wire with a flush cut on the other end of the bead stack and make another hairpin bend, securing the beads in place. (This completes the first pivot of the bracelet.)

4 Turn the 2 inner spacer bars to the right and the 2 outer spacer bars to the left. Use the cut end of the wire to string 1 seed bead, one 4mm daisy spacer, the end hole of 1 new spacer bar, 1 rondelle, the end hole (far right) of 1 inner spacer bar, one 6mm bicone, the end hole (far right) of the second inner spacer bar, 1 rondelle, the end hole of 1 new spacer bar, one 4mm spacer, and 1 seed bead. Repeat Step 3.

5 Turn the 2 outer spacer bars added in Step 4 to the right. Use the cut end of the wire to string 1 seed bead, one 4mm daisy spacer, the end hole (far right) of 1 outer spacer bar, 1 rondelle, the end hole of 1 spacer bar, one 6mm bicone, the end hole of 1 spacer bar, 1 rondelle, the end hole (far right) of the second outer spacer bar, one 4mm daisy spacer, and 1 seed bead. Repeat Step 3.

6 ***Note:*** *The long and short center wires are decorative and not structural, with the wire passing through the center holes of the spacer bars.* Flush-cut one end of the 22g wire. String 1 seed bead, one 3mm daisy spacer, the center hole of 1 outer spacer bar, one 4mm daisy spacer, one 3mm bicone, two 4mm bicones, one 3mm bicone, one 4mm daisy spacer, the center hole of the second outer spacer bar, one 3mm daisy spacer, and 1 seed bead. Repeat Step 3.

7 Use the cut end of the 22g wire to string 1 seed bead, one 3mm daisy spacer, the center hole of 1 inner spacer bar, one 3mm bicone, 1 seed bead, one 3mm bicone, the center hole of the second inner spacer bar, one 3mm daisy spacer, and 1 seed bead. Repeat Step 3. For the center short wire of the bracelet, add one 4mm daisy spacer to each side, next to the 3mm spacers.

8 Continue adding links after the center short wire, alternating a pivot, long center, pivot, short center, and so on, until the bracelet reaches the desired length. Both ends should either be narrow (2 inner spacer bars), or wide (2 outer spacer bars). Using the cut end of the 20g wire, string 1 seed bead, one 4mm daisy spacer, the last hole of the end spacer bar, 1 rondelle, one 4mm daisy spacer, 1 seed bead, three 4mm daisy spacers, 1 seed bead, one 4mm daisy spacer, 1 rondelle, the last hole of the second outer spacer bar, one 4mm daisy spacer, and 1 seed bead. Repeat Step 3. Repeat this entire step on the opposite end of the bracelet.

9 Open all 4 jump rings. Slide 1 jump ring around each of the seed beads in the center of the end stack on one end of the bracelet. Attach one side of the clasp; close the jump rings. Repeat on the other end of the bracelet.

Ancient Artifacts

Layer a triangular toggle ring over a hammered metal blank for earrings that evoke the rich treasures uncovered at archeological digs.

TIP

Use one leftover bar half of one clasp to create your own custom clasp with a washer as Erin did in her Washer Woman necklace (page 62).

ERIN STROTHER

Materials

- 2 brecciated jasper 7×4mm rondelles
- 2 amber 4×3mm crystal rondelles
- 2 turquoise ceramic 15×8mm saucers
- 2 copper 5mm spacers
- 8 brass 8mm wavy discs
- 2 brass triangle 25mm blanks
- 2 copper 2" (5.1 cm) eye pins
- 2 brass 6mm jump rings
- 2 silver-plated 15mm triangle toggle clasps
- 2 silver-plated beaded ear wires

Tools

Round-nose pliers
2 pairs chain- or flat-nose pliers
1.8mm metal hole-punch pliers
Wire cutters
Bench block
Ball-peen hammer
Permanent marker
Liver of sulfur (optional)
Polishing cloth (optional)

Techniques *(see page 130)*

Hammering ▪ Hole punching ▪ Jump rings ▪ Simple loops ▪ Oxidizing (optional)

Finished Size

2¾" (7 cm)

Variation

Use guitar-pick-shaped brass blanks with turquoise chips, smoky quartz nuggets, pearls, and silver spacers for a slightly softer version.

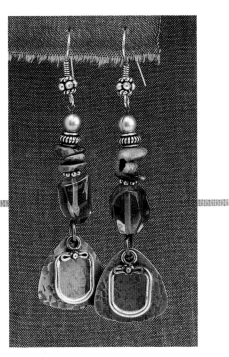

1 Use the ball end of the ball-peen hammer to texture the triangle blanks on the bench block. Use the marker to mark the top corner of the triangle where the hole will be punched. Use the hole-punch pliers to punch the holes. Use a liver of sulfur solution to darken the brass, if desired. Use a polishing cloth to bring up some shiny highlights.

2 Attach the ring part of the toggle clasp to the triangle blank using 1 jump ring.

3 Use 1 eye pin to string 3 brass wavy discs, 1 ceramic saucer, 1 wavy disc, 1 jasper rondelle, 1 copper spacer, and 1 crystal. Trim the wire and form a simple loop. Attach the bottom loop of the eye pin to the jump ring from Step 2. Attach the top loop to the ear wire.

4 Repeat Steps 1–3 for the second earring.

Poet Laureate

Inspired by an ancient symbol of honor, a brass laurel circle pendant adorned with wire-wrapped red pearl flowers, layered in front of a handpainted teal circle, hangs from a custom filigree bail.

TIP

Bail-making pliers allow you to make larger curves, such as those used in this bail. If you don't have bail-making pliers, use the largest part of your round-nose pliers instead.

MICHELLE MACH

Materials

- 4 cranberry 4mm freshwater pearls
- 1 teal 25mm brass polka-dotted circle pendant
- 1 brass 15×21mm filigree diamond connector
- 1 brass 36mm fern laurel circle connector
- 4 brass 13.5mm open 6-petal fairy-petal flowers
- 2 brass 4×12mm foldover cord ends
- 3 bright brass 2" (5.1 cm) head pins
- 1 dark brass 2" (5.1 cm) head pin
- 5 brass 4mm jump rings
- 1 brass 10mm jump ring
- 1 brass 11×17mm spring-ring clasp
- 42" (1.1 m) of burgundy 2mm silk cord
- 1 brass 5×8mm etched chain link
- Jeweler's glue (optional)

Tools

Round-nose pliers
2 pairs of chain- or flat-nose pliers
1.8mm metal hole-punch pliers
Scissors
2mm/4mm bail-making pliers (optional)

Techniques *(see page 130)*

Hole punching ▪ Gluing ▪ Jump rings ▪ Wire wrapping

Finished Size

22" (55.9 cm)

Variation

If you substitute a smaller clasp that fits through the bail (such as a small lobster clasp), you can wear the pendant on different chains and cords.

> *Wear your jewelry. Often that's the only way to know if a bracelet is too heavy or the clasp on a necklace won't stay closed.*
> —Michelle Mach

1 Use 1 bright brass head pin to string 1 pearl, the center of 1 flower, and the loop in the tip of 1 leaf on the circle connector. Wrap the head pin around the top of 1 flower petal. Skip the next petal and wrap the head pin round the next petal. Repeat. Wrap the remaining head pin around the base of the loop on the tip of leaf. Repeat this entire step twice to add a total of 3 pearl flowers to the leaf connector.

2 Place the circle connector on top of the teal circle. Use the hole punch to punch 3 holes in the teal circle in between the 3 rings on the outside edge of the connector. Use one 4mm jump ring to attach 1 hole in the teal circle to the edge the connector. Repeat twice. Set the pendant aside.

3 Use bail-making pliers to bend the diamond filigree connector in half, forming a bail, and leaving a ⅛" (3.2 mm) gap between the ends. Use the chain link to connect 1 ring on the circle connector to the bottom 2 holes of the diamond filigree bail.

4 Cut the cord in half. Use both cords to string the diamond filigree bail. Place both cord ends on one side of the necklace into 1 foldover cord end. If desired, dab jeweler's glue inside the foldover cord end before closing it with chain- or flat-nose pliers. Let dry. Repeat with both cords on the other side end of the necklace.

5 Use the dark brass head pin to string 1 pearl, the center of 1 flower, and the center of the spring-ring clasp. Wrap the head pin around the alternating petals of the flower as you did in Step 1. Wrap the remaining head pin around the clasp, avoiding the area near the clasp's opening and closing lever. Use one 4mm jump ring to attach the clasp to 1 foldover cord end. Use one 4mm jump ring to attach the other foldover cord end to one 10mm jump ring.

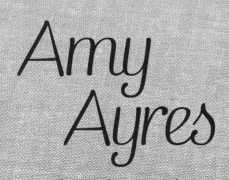

Amy Ayres

Just as dancers such as Amy Ayres can move in amazing ways, so, too, can brass components. Create a bangle with large pieces of brass and turn a folded piece of filigree into a custom clasp.

DENISE YEZBAK MOORE

Materials

- 6 fuchsia 8mm round shell rounds
- 1 brass 28×16mm hummingbird pendant
- 1 brass 35×14mm music note pendant
- 1 brass 53×12mm feather pendant
- 1 brass 88×18mm feather pendant
- 1 brass 16×30mm 3-hole nouveau filigree connector
- 1 brass 18×14mm magnolia-leaf bead cap
- 7 brass 1" (2.5 cm) eye pins
- 1 brass 9.5mm round etched jump ring
- 6 brass 5mm jump rings
- 2 brass 10mm 16-gauge jump rings
- 2 brass 7mm jump rings
- 36" (91.4 cm) of fuchsia sari silk
- Superglue

Tools

Round-nose pliers
2 pairs of chain- or flat-nose pliers
Wire cutters
Scissors
Bracelet mandrel

Techniques *(see page 130)*

Braiding ▪ Filigree forming ▪ Gluing
Jump rings ▪ Overhand knots ▪
Simple loops

Finished Size

7¼" (18.4 cm)

Variation

Lorelei Eurto's elegant necklace features tiny pearls and sheer gold-threaded ribbon along with the same feather that Denise used..

1 Gently shape the large brass feather around the bracelet mandrel until it fits the curve of your wrist snugly.

2 Use round-nose pliers to form a simple loop with the quill of the large feather. Use a 5mm jump ring to connect the 9.5mm etched jump ring to the hole in the end of the large feather.

3 Use 1 eye pin to string 1 fuchsia round. Trim the wire and form a simple loop. Repeat 5 times, connecting the loops together in a chain. Connect one 7mm jump ring to one end of the chain. Set aside.

4 Using round-nose pliers, grasp the filigree connector ½" (1.3 cm) from the 1-hole tip and bend it back into a inverted U shape. Measure ¼" (6.4 mm) from the tip and bend the tip back upward. Pinch the second bend closed. Set the clasp aside.

5 Cut the silk into three 12" (30.5 cm) pieces. Bring the tails together on one end and string them through one 10mm jump ring. Form a simple overhand knot around the jump ring, trim the short tails, and dab the knot with glue to secure.

6 Braid the 3 strands of silk to a length of 3" (7.6 cm). String another 10mm jump ring and form a simple overhand knot around the jump ring. Trim the tails to ½" (1.3 cm) and fray the ends. Dab the knot with glue to secure. Let dry.

7 Using round-nose pliers, gently bend the tips of the bead cap petals up to a 90° angle and open the bead cap slightly. String 1 eye pin through the bead cap and form a simple loop. Connect the 10mm jump ring from Step 5 and the 7mm jump ring from Step 3 to the simple loop. Close the bead cap around the knot and chain.

8 Use two 5mm jump rings to connect the 10mm jump ring on the other end of the silk braid to the free side of the filigree clasp.

9 Use one 7mm brass jump ring to string the loop on the large feather and the eye-pin loop on top of the bead cap; close the ring. Connect one 5mm jump ring to the 7mm jump ring. Use one 5mm jump ring to string the small feather and the previous 5mm jump ring; close the ring. Use one 5mm jump ring to string the hummingbird and music note and the previous 5mm jump ring; close the ring.

Branching Out

A leafy spacer bar and a tiny bird bead become the focal point of this soothing, soft green-and-silver necklace.

TIP

Adding an extension chain allows the wearer to adjust the length of the necklace. The wearer simply attaches the lobster clasp to any chain link.

CINDY WIMMER

Materials

- 1 polymer clay 36×23mm green oval pendant
- 4 green 10×7mm rutilated quartz briolettes
- 4 green 4mm faceted aventurine rounds
- 13 khaki AB 4mm crystal rounds
- 4 honey jade 6mm faceted rounds
- 123 green 3mm aventurine rounds
- 1 sterling silver 6mm bird
- 1 sterling silver 20.5×10.5mm triple-strand twig **spacer bar**
- 1 sterling silver 20-gauge 2" (5.1 cm) head pin
- 17 sterling silver 24-gauge 1½" (3.8 cm) head pins
- 3 sterling silver 7mm jump rings
- 2 sterling silver 3.5mm crimp covers
- 2 sterling silver 2mm crimp tubes
- 1 sterling silver 14mm lobster clasp with attached 4mm jump ring
- 24" (61 cm) of 22-gauge sterling silver wire
- 20" (50.8 cm) of .014 flexible beading wire
- 12" (30.5 cm) of sterling silver 5mm flat cable chain

Tools

Round-nose pliers
Chain-nose pliers
Flat-nose pliers
Crimping pliers
Wire cutters
Liver of sulfur gel (optional)
Fine steel wool (#0000; optional)
Polishing cloth (optional)

Techniques *(see page 130)*

Crimp covers ▪ Crimping ▪ Jump rings ▪ Stringing ▪ Wrapped loops ▪ Oxidizing (optional)

Finished Size

16½" (41.9 cm)

1 Oxidize the chain, jump rings, bird bead, clasp, and head pins in a liver of sulfur solution if desired. Rinse and dry. Remove the excess oxidization with fine steel wool. Polish with a polishing cloth.

2 Cut the chain into two 26-link pieces, four 7-link pieces, and two 2-link pieces. Attach the jump ring on the lobster clasp to one end of one 26-link chain. Attach one 7mm jump ring to the other 26-link chain. Attach 2 more 7mm jump rings to the previous jump ring to create an extension chain. Set aside.

3 Use the 2" (5.1 cm) head pin to string the bird bead and the center hole in the branch spacer bar. Create a large (about ¼" [6 mm]) wrapped loop that attaches to the polymer clay pendant.

4 Use 3½" (8.9 cm) of silver wire to form a wrapped loop that attaches to a leaf on one end of the spacer bar.

5 String 1 briolette and form a wrapped loop that attaches to a 7-link chain. Use 1 head pin to string 1 crystal round; form a wrapped loop that attaches to the chain, 3 links from the briolette; repeat. Create 1 crystal dangle that attaches to the chain, 4 links from the briolette.

6 Use 1 head pin to string one 4mm aventurine round; form a wrapped loop that attaches to the end of the chain. Use 2½" (6.4 cm) of silver wire to form a wrapped loop that also attaches to the end of the chain. String 1 jade round; form a wrapped loop that attaches to a 2-link chain.

7 Cut 3½" (8.9 cm) of silver wire and repeat Steps 5 and 6, attaching the second wrapped loop of the second jade round to the opposite end of the 26-link chain attached to the lobster clasp.

8 Repeat Steps 4–7 to complete the other side of the necklace, attaching the second wrapped loop of the final jade round to the opposite end of the 26-link chain attached to the extension chain. Use 1 head pin to string 1 crystal round; form a wrapped loop that attaches to the free end of the extension chain.

9 Use the flexible beading wire to string 1 crimp tube and the jump ring of the lobster clasp. Pass the wire back through the tube and crimp the tube with crimping pliers. Trim the flexible beading wire. String all remaining aventurine rounds, 1 crimp tube, and the first jump ring of the extension chain. Pass the wire back through the tube and crimp. Trim the flexible beading wire. Cover each crimp tube with 1 crimp cover.

Cognificent

Mimic the look of rivets with head pins and
simple loops in this steampunk cuff studded
with brass, gunmetal, and copper gears.

TIP

If you'd like the
propeller to spin,
make sure that you
do not create any tall
stacks of beads in the
adjacent holes.

TIP

If the gears feel loose
after you finish your
simple or double
loop, wrap 2–3"
(5.1–7.6 cm) of craft
wire around the base
of the gear and tuck
the ends in.

MICHELLE MACH

Materials

- 1 silver-colored brass 34mm cuff with 41 holes
- 1 matte copper 5mm fire-polished glass round
- 2 copper 3mm rounds
- 1 brass 3mm cube bead
- 1 brass 3.5mm spacer
- 1 brass 6mm daisy spacer
- 3 copper-plated 6mm daisy spacers
- 2 copper-plated 4mm hexagon spacers
- 1 copper-plated 7×5mm spacer
- 1 dark brass 8×4mm saucer
- 1 brass 18mm propeller
- 1 brass 6mm sprocket
- 2 brass 16mm gears
- 2 brass 20mm gears
- 1 dark brass 29mm gear
- 1 antique brass 12mm 3-hole gear
- 1 copper 16mm gear
- 1 copper 16mm open 5-hole gear
- 2 antiqued copper 12mm 3-hole gears
- 1 antiqued copper 21mm open 3-hole gear
- 1 gunmetal 20mm gear
- 1 gunmetal 13mm 4-hole gear
- 1 gunmetal 21mm open 3-hole gear
- 1 gunmetal 6mm fluted bead cap
- 1 gunmetal 8mm textured bead cap
- 1 brass 4mm hive bead cap
- 2 copper 12mm etched bead caps
- 8 brass 2" (5.1 cm) 20-gauge head pins
- 3 copper 2" (5.1 cm) 20-gauge head pins
- 2 silver-plated 2" (5.1 cm) 20-gauge head pins
- 26-gauge bronze craft wire (optional)

Tools

Round-nose pliers
Wire cutters
Painter's tape (optional)

Techniques *(see page 130)*

Double simple loops ■ Simple loops ■ Wire wrapping (optional)

Finished Size

7½" (19.1 cm)

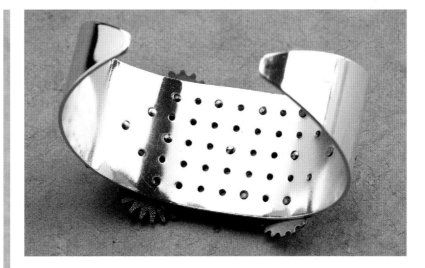

1 Beginning in the center of the cuff, use 1 brass head pin to string the middle hole. String the 29mm brass gear, one 20mm brass gear, the gunmetal 3-hole gear, 1 copper daisy spacer, and the 8mm gunmetal bead cap. Hold the stack flush against the cuff; form a double simple loop.

2 Use 1 silver-plated head pin to string the hole on the far left. String 1 copper bead cap and 1 copper daisy spacer; form a double simple loop.

3 Continue adding stacks of gears and beads on head pins, finishing with either simple or double simple loops. Top row, from left to right: 20mm brass gear, 21mm antique copper 3-hole gear, brass cube bead; matte copper fire-polished round; 7×5 copper spacer, etched bead cap, copper daisy spacer, hexagon spacer; 16mm brass gear, 12mm copper 3-hole gear, hexagon spacer. Middle row, after the copper bead cap: 16mm copper gear, gunmetal 4-hole gear, brass beehive bead cap. Skip the large center added in Step 1. Brass daisy spacer, brass saucer; brass sprocket, copper round; brass propeller. Bottom row: 16mm brass gear, antique brass 3-hole gear, copper round; 12mm antique copper 3-hole gear, 3.5mm brass spacer; 20mm gunmetal gear, copper 5-hole gear, and gunmetal fluted bead cap.

Variation

Use a brass filigree cuff to showcase layers of metal flowers, bead caps, blue glass rondelles, and faceted-amethyst rounds for a feminine cuff.

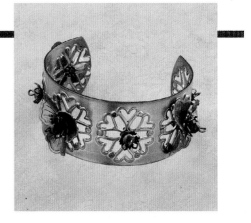

Dalle de Verre

Seed beads in shades of royal, denim, and azure combine with ball-chain connectors to create a stained-glass effect. *Dalle de verre*, French for "glass slab," is a glass-art technique often found in old churches.

MICHELLE MACH

Materials

- 2 cobalt blue 7mm ceramic rounds
- 2 denim blue 4mm shell rounds
- 3 blue goldstone 4mm rounds
- 8 copper 4mm fire-polished glass rounds
- 2 Montana blue 6×4mm faceted-glass rondelles
- 64 blue 4mm crystal pearls
- 2 matte cobalt blue 3×2mm glass discs
- 90 (about 1 gram) assorted blue size 11° seed beads
- 21 copper-plated ball-chain connectors
- 4 copper-plated 5-hole spacer bars
- 4 copper-plated 6mm daisy spacers
- 5 copper 2" (5 cm) head pins
- 2 copper 4mm jump rings
- 4 brass 4mm jump rings
- 9 copper-plated 6mm jump rings
- 2 copper 2mm crimp tubes
- 2 copper 3mm crimp covers
- 1 blue 15mm enameled toggle clasp
- 18" (45.5 cm) of .019 flexible beading wire
- 14" (35.5 cm) of copper-plated 4mm circle chain

Tools

Round-nose pliers
2 pairs of chain- or flat-nose pliers
Crimping pliers
Wire cutters

Techniques (see page 130)

Crimping ■ Crimp covers ■ Jump rings ■ Simple loops ■ Stringing

Finished Size

16" (40.6 cm)

Variation

Use graph paper to map out patterns and fill the clasps with strategically placed beads, rather than the random assortment used here.

1 Use 1 head pin to string the outer left hole of 1 spacer bar, 1 hole of 1 ball-chain connector, 4 seed beads that will fit inside the connector, and the other hole of the connector. Repeat this step twice adding the components to the same head pin. String the outer left hole of 1 final spacer bar and 1 blue goldstone round; form a simple loop.

2 Repeat Step 1 four more times to fill the remaining holes on the spacer bars. For the second and fourth strands, replace the blue goldstone with 1 pearl. Attach each simple loop to 1 copper 6mm jump ring. Set aside.

3 Use 1 copper 6mm jump ring to attach 1 copper 6mm jump ring to one half of the toggle clasp. Use 1 brass 4mm jump ring to attach the previous copper 6mm jump ring to 1 brass 4mm jump ring. Repeat this entire step for the other half of the toggle clasp.

4 Attach the previous 4mm jump ring to one end of the chain. Repeat for the other end of the chain.

5 Attach 1 copper 4mm jump ring to the copper 6mm jump ring directly attached to one half of the toggle clasp. Use the flexible beading wire to string 1 crimp tube and the previous 4mm jump ring. Pass the wire back through the tube and crimp the tube with crimping pliers. Cover the tube using 1 copper crimp cover.

6 String 3 seed beads, 1 copper fire-polished round, 1 daisy spacer, and 29 pearls. String {1 hole of 1 ball-chain connector, 4 seed beads, the second hole of the connector, and 1 pearl} 3 times, omitting the final pearl. String 1 shell round, 1 Montana blue rondelle, 1 ceramic round, 1 daisy spacer, and 1 matte cobalt blue disc.

7 String {1 copper fire-polished round and 1 jump ring on the pendant} 5 times. String 1 copper fire-polished round.

8 Repeat Step 6, reversing the stringing sequence. Repeat Step 5 using the other half of the toggle clasp.

Maya

Stacks of split rings not only add texture to this Mayan-inspired necklace, but their spring-like construction protects delicate ribbon from snagging as an open jump ring might.

TIP

If you can't find the right size or color ribbon, make your own by cutting a strip from a larger piece of fabric.

ERIN SIEGEL

Materials

- 1 Aztec-red 5-hole 90×5mm crescent ceramic pendant
- 4 opaque turquoise 6mm glass rounds
- 3 opaque turquoise 4mm glass rounds
- 7 copper 3mm faceted cornerless cubes
- 3 Aztec-red 14×13mm rhombus ceramic charms
- 94 antique copper 9mm split rings
- 4 antique copper 3" (7.6 cm) head pins
- 1 antique copper 16mm toggle clasp
- 36" (91.4 cm) of antique copper ¾" (1.9 cm) douppioni silk ribbon
- 20" (50.8 cm) of antique copper 24-gauge wire

Tools

Round-nose pliers
Chain-nose pliers
Wire cutters
Scissors
Ruler

Techniques *(see page 130)*

Simple loops ▪ Stringing ▪ Wire wrapping ▪ Wrapped loops

Finished Size

18" (45.7 cm)

Variation

Instead of stacking the split rings on the sides of a necklace, use them as decorative spacers in between multiple charms or pendants.

1 Use 1 head pin to string 1 copper cube and 1 turquoise 6mm round; form a wrapped loop. Set aside.

2 Use 1 head pin to string 1 copper cube and 1 turquoise 4mm round. String the head pin through one of the holes in the crescent pendant from the top to the bottom. String 1 turquoise 6mm round and 1 copper bead; form a simple loop. Attach 1 rhombus charm to the simple loop. Repeat this entire step 2 more times.

3 Use one 18" (45.7 cm) piece of silk ribbon to string 1 hole on one end of the crescent pendant. Use both ribbon ends to string 45 split rings.

4 Use both ribbons ends to string 1 split ring. Keeping the ribbon ends together, fold 3" (7.6 cm) over the split ring. Wrap 10" (25.4 cm) of copper wire around the ribbon to secure. Tuck in the wire ends. Trim the ribbon tails to 1" (2.5 cm).

5 Use 1 head pin to string 1 turquoise 6mm bead and attach it to the split ring in Step 4 with a wrapped loop.

6 Use 1 split ring to attach the split ring from Step 4 to one half of the toggle clasp.

7 Repeat Steps 3, 4, and 6 to complete the other side of the necklace.

Tip

If you decide to substitute jump rings for the split rings, use heavy-gauge rings that are less likely to come open accidentally.

Wish Me Luck

Use an open-backed bezel like a shadow box to house a special art bead. Wrapping tiny faceted carnelian rondelles around the bezel adds drama to the pendant.

TIP

If you don't own memory-wire cutters, use hardware-store cutters. Cutting hard steel wire with your good jewelry cutters will ruin them.

ERIN PRAIS-HINTZ

Materials

- 1 blue 18×32mm ceramic WISH heart pendant
- 1 moonstone 10.5×19.5mm faceted inverted teardrop
- 12 citrine AB rough-cut 11–16×4–7mm faceted nuggets (B)
- 28 carnelian AB 4×2mm faceted rondelles (C)
- 6 aquamarine 7×17.8mm center-drilled faceted marquise beads (D)
- 8 green 9mm faceted freshwater pearls (E)
- 12 silver-plated 4.5mm daisy spacers (F)
- 1 white bronze 29×50mm open-backed shield bezel
- 38 brass 9.5mm etched jump rings
  2 silver-plated 2mm crimp tubes
- 1 silver-plated 8×19.5mm hook clasp
- 72" (1.8 m) of dark annealed 28-gauge steel wire
- 11" (27.9 cm) of .019 flexible beading wire
- 8" (20.3 cm) of antique silver-plated unsoldered 5.7mm rolo chain
- Renaissance Wax

Tools

Round-nose pliers
2 pairs of chain-nose pliers
Crimping pliers
Memory-wire cutters
Wire cutters
Fine steel wool (#0000)
Paper towel

Techniques *(see page 130)*

Chain maille ▪ Crimping ▪ Double-loop briolette wrapped loop ▪ Jump rings ▪ Stringing ▪ Wire wrapping

Finished Size

18" (45.7 cm)

Variation

Suspend a beautiful gemstone bead inside the bezel instead of an art bead for an earthier look.

1. Use memory-wire cutters to cut the steel wire into one 24" (61 cm) and one 48" (1.2 m) length. Run the wire between the steel wool to clean it and use a small amount of Renaissance Wax between your fingers to coat the wire. Remove the excess wax and black coating from the wire with a paper towel.

2. Use the 24" (61 cm) wire to string the moonstone teardrop. Form a double-loop briolette wrapped loop by bringing both sides of the wire together at the top of the bead. Use round-nose pliers to make a wrapped loop with both wires and then wrap the entire top of the bead with both wires. Tuck in the tail ends. Set aside.

3. Starting at the tip of the bezel frame, wrap the middle of the 48" (1.2 m) wire around the frame 2–3 times to secure. Use 1 wire tail to string 1 carnelian rondelle and wrap it onto the outside of the frame. Wrap the frame 2–3 more times and add another carnelian rondelle. Continue this pattern, adding 10 carnelian rondelles to the outside of one side of the frame. Use the second wire tail to repeat this pattern on the other side of the frame. End with both tail wires at the top of the frame.

4. Center the ceramic heart pendant under the top of the frame and use the tail wires to wrap the loop of the pendant and the top of the frame several times to secure. Tuck in the tails.

5. Attach 1 jump ring to the top loop of the bezel; close the jump ring. Use 1 jump ring to string the moonstone dangle and the bottom loop of the bezel; close the jump ring.

6. Connect 2 jump rings together. Place the jump rings on top of each other and use 1 more jump ring to string the connected jump ring pair, forming a chain-maille rosette (A). Close the jump ring. Repeat for a total of 10 rosettes (or 10A).

7. Connect 2 jump rings together; repeat.

8. Use the flexible beading wire to string 1 crimp tube and 1 jump ring pair from Step 7. Bring the flexible beading wire back through the tube and crimp with crimping pliers.

9. String the following: 2A, 1B, 1C, 1B, 1C, 1B, 1A, 1E, 1F, 1D, 1F, 1E, 1F, 1D, 1F, 1E, 1F, 1D, 1F, 1E, 1A, 1B, 1C, 1B, 1C, 1B, and 1A.

10. String the jump ring attached to the top of the bezel and repeat Step 9 in reverse order. Repeat Step 8.

11. Separate the chain into two 4" (10.2 cm) pieces, opening and closing the chain links as you would jump rings. Open 1 link on one end of 1 chain and attach it to the jump ring pair on one end of the beaded section; close the link. Repeat to attach the second chain to the opposite side of the necklace.

12. Use 1 jump ring to attach the hook clasp to the free end of 1 chain. Attach 1 jump ring to the free end of the second chain.

A Passel of Tassels

Jump rings tied to linen cords add a touch of whimsy to these sunny earrings.

VARIATION

Create a second pair of earrings with light blue, yellow, and gray cords that accent handmade ceramic and glass beads.

LORELEI EURTO

Materials

- 2 orange 5×20mm lampwork-glass donuts
- 21" (53.3 cm) of light rust 4-ply waxed linen cord
- 21" (53.3 cm) of salmon 4-ply waxed linen cord
- 21" (53.3 cm) of orange 4-ply waxed linen cord
- 12" (30.5 cm) of gold 4-ply waxed linen cord
- 4 brass 7mm jump rings
- 4 brass 15mm jump rings
- 24 brass 4.5mm jump rings
- 2 brass 20×10mm ear wires

Tools

2 pairs of chain- or flat-nose pliers
Scissors

Techniques *(see page 130)*

Jump rings ▪ Overhand knots

Finished Size

3¼" (8.3 cm)

Tip

Make sure that the 4.5mm jump rings are tightly closed before tying them to the linen cords.

"Keeping an organized studio is the top priority when running a jewelry business. Grouping like materials in storage drawers or bins helps me find what I'm looking for. I have drawers for lampworked glass, ceramics, Lucite, metals, ribbons, and mixed media and then within the drawers, I organize by color. Keep that label maker handy as it's a great way to label beads with artists' names, material, or price." —Lorelei Eurto

1. Cut all of the light rust, salmon, and orange cords into 3½" (8.9 cm) pieces. Separate the cords into 2 bunches with 3 strands of each color.

2. Thread 1 bunch through a 15mm jump ring and pull the ends together, folding the cords in half.

3. Cut the gold cord into two 6" (15.2 cm) pieces. Use 1 gold cord to wrap around the orange tassel tightly about 8–9 times; tie an overhand knot. Trim the excess gold cord with scissors leaving ¼" (6.4 mm) tails.

4. Tie 12 brass 4.5mm jump rings onto 12 strands around the exterior of the tassel, at varying lengths, using overhand knots. Trim the tassel so all the strands are about 1½" (3.8 cm) long.

5. Open the 15mm jump ring attached to the tassel and string one 7mm jump ring, 1 lampwork donut, and one 7mm jump ring; close the 15mm jump ring. Open a second 15mm jump ring and string the same 7mm jump ring, donut, and 7mm jump ring; close the 15mm jump ring. Attach 1 ear wire to the top 15mm jump ring.

6. Repeat Steps 2–5 for the second earring.

Sadie's Secret

The secret's out! Create two feminine necklaces inspired by the designer's favorite vintage shop by using multiple magnetic clasps that look like round metal beads to the casual observer.

TIP

Caution: Magnetic clasps should not be worn by people with pacemakers. Substitute round, bead-shaped box clasps to achieve the same look.

ERIN SIEGEL

Materials

- 1 brass 48×40mm filigree butterfly
- 6 amethyst 8mm pressed-glass rounds
- 2 light Colorado 8mm rhinestone rounds
- 13 white 12×7mm teardrop glass pearls
- 15 g of metallic bronze 4mm magatama seed beads
- 12 brass 6mm filigree bead caps
- 2 brass 14×23mm tulip bead caps
- 4 brass 8mm round magnetic clasps
- 8' (2.4 m) of antique brass 20-gauge wire
- 15' (4.6 m) of Victoria pink 4-ply Irish waxed linen cord

Tools

Round-nose pliers
Chain-nose pliers
Wire cutters
Scissors
Ruler

Techniques (see page 130)

Double-wrapped loops ▪ Overhand knots ▪ Slipknot ▪ Stringing ▪ Wire wrapping ▪ Wrapped loops

Finished Size

20½" (52.1 cm)

Tip

Test the clasps before finishing your necklace to make sure you've aligned the correct ends together.

1 Use 4" (10.2 cm) of wire to form a wrapped loop that attaches to one half of 1 magnetic clasp (A). String 1 pearl and form a wrapped loop. Use 4" (10.2 cm) of wire to form a wrapped loop that connects to the previous wrapped loop, string 1 pearl, and form a wrapped loop; repeat 11 times. Attach one half of another magnetic clasp (B) to the last wrapped loop, making sure the magnetic halves on each end of the pearl chain do *not* attract.

2 Form a wrapped loop on one end of a 4" (10.2 cm) piece of wire. Repeat and set aside. Use five 3' (91.4 cm) pieces of waxed linen cord to string 1 wrapped loop to the center of the cords. Fold the cords in half and form an overhand knot with all the cords.

3 Use 1 cord to string 3 seed beads. Measure ½" (1.3 cm) from the previous knot and form an overhand knot, capturing the 3 seed beads within the knot. Repeat 11 times down the length of cord. Repeat this entire step for the remaining 9 cords.

4 Use all 10 cords to string the other wrapped loop and form a slipknot with all the cords together. Trim the ends.

5 String 1 tulip bead cap onto 1 wire, covering the knot, and form a double-wrapped loop that connects to the remaining half of magnetic clasp A. Repeat this entire step for the other side, connecting the remaining half of magnetic clasp B.

6 Use 4" (10.2 cm) of wire to form a wrapped loop that attaches to one side of the filigree butterfly. String 1 rhinestone round and form a wrapped loop. *Use 4" (10.2 cm) of wire to form a wrapped loop that connects to the previous wrapped loop. String 1 bead cap, 1 amethyst round and 1 bead cap; form a wrapped loop.** Repeat from * to ** 2 more times, attaching the last wrapped loop to one half of 1 magnetic clasp (C). Repeat this entire step on the other side of the filigree butterfly, attaching the last wrapped loop to one half of 1 magnetic clasp (D). Make sure that the attached clasp halves do not attract to each other. **Note:** *The magnets on the pearl chain will connect to the butterfly section and also to the clasps on the beaded strands. The beaded strands will not connect to the butterfly section.*

Key West

Dark wood beads strung across a bracelet-cuff-turned-pendant look like a parrot's tail feathers, while the orange and yellow wood beads echo the colors of the dazzling sunsets of this quirky Florida town.

TIP
While you may be able to wrap the wire on the pendant with your fingers, sometimes using the tip of your chain-nose pliers can make it easier to make a tight wrap.

TIP
Covering crimps with jump rings rather than crimp covers adds a playful feel.

MICHELLE MACH

Materials

- 5 black ebony wood 8–11×29–34mm feathers
- 16 orange redwood 5mm rounds
- 43 orange redwood 8mm rounds
- 84 yellow nangka wood 6mm rounds
- 2 bronze 8mm porcelain rounds
- 2 antiqued copper 6mm rounds
- 2 antiqued copper 4mm rounds
- 4 mocha 12mm large-hole porcelain discs
- 8 brass 7×4mm saucers
- 2 brass 5mm daisy spacers
- 8 copper size 11° metal seed beads
- 1 brass 68mm hoop bracelet blank
- 2 copper 5×9mm lobster clasps
- 1 brass 2" (5.1 cm) eye pin
- 2 copper 5mm jump rings
- 22 brass 4mm jump rings
- 2 copper 2mm crimp tubes
- 6" (15.2 cm) of bronze 20-gauge craft wire
- 48" (1.2 m) of .018 flexible beading wire

Tools

Round-nose pliers
2 pairs of chain- or flat-nose pliers
Crimping pliers
Wire cutters
Bead stops

Techniques *(see page 130)*

Crimping ■ Jump rings ■ Simple loops ■ Stringing ■ Wire wrapping

Finished Size

18½" (47 cm)

Variation

Remove the pendant and connect the lobster clasps to each other or a piece of chain for a simple two-strand necklace.

1 Use the craft wire to wrap the upper left midpoint of the bracelet blank 3 times. String 1 copper seed bead, five 4mm jump rings, one 5mm orange round, 1 copper seed bead, 1 wood feather, 1 copper seed bead, one 5mm orange round, 1 copper seed bead, 3 wood feathers, 1 copper seed bead, one 5mm orange round, 1 copper seed bead, 1 wood feather, 1 copper seed bead, one 5mm orange round, 1 copper seed bead, and five 4mm jump rings. Wrap the wire around the upper right midpoint of the bracelet blank 3 times. Trim the wire and pinch in the ends with chain-nose pliers.

2 Use 1 eye pin to string the left hole of the bracelet blank. String one 8mm orange round, 1 saucer, 1 yellow round, 1 saucer, one 8mm orange round, and the right hole of the bracelet blank. Form a simple loop. Attach 1 copper jump ring to the eye of the eye pin and attach another jump ring to the simple loop. Set the pendant aside.

3 Cut the flexible beading wire in half.

4 Attach 1 brass jump ring to 1 lobster clasp. Use both flexible beading wires to string 1 crimp tube and the previous jump ring. Pass both wires back through the tube and crimp the tube using crimping pliers. String 5 brass jump rings over the tube.

5 Use both flexible beading wires to string one 4mm copper round, one 6mm copper round, one 5mm orange round, 3 saucers, 1 daisy spacer, 1 bronze round, and 2 mocha discs.

6 Place a bead stop on the end of 1 wire. Use the other wire to string 83 yellow rounds. Place a bead stop on the end of this wire. Remove the bead stop from the first wire and string five 5mm orange rounds and 41 orange 8mm rounds. Remove the bead stop. Repeat Step 5, reversing the stringing sequence. Repeat Step 4.

7 Attach the lobster clasps to the copper jump rings on either side of the pendant.

Constellation

Create a delicate chain reminiscent of a starry night by combining head pins, eye pins, and smooth crystal pearls in shades of gray and black.

TIP

If you substitute freshwater pearls, you may need to use a bead reamer to gently enlarge the holes to fit the head pins.

ERIN STROTHER

Materials

- 5 light gray 8mm crystal pearls
- 11 dark gray 6mm crystal pearls
- 8 black 6mm crystal pearls
- 12 silver-plated 20-gauge 2" (5.1 cm) head pins
- 14 silver-plated 1" (2.5 cm) eye pins
- 4 silver-plated 4mm jump rings
- 24 silver-plated 6mm jump rings
- 1 silver-plated 12mm toggle clasp

Tools

Round-nose pliers
2 pairs of chain- or flat-nose pliers
Wire cutters

Finished Size

16½" (41.9 cm)

Techniques *(see page 130)*

Jump rings ▪ Simple loops

"Try turning something on its side or upside down. Use unexpected combinations like something industrial paired with something polished or sparkly."
—Erin Strother

1 String 1 black pearl onto an eye pin. Trim the wire and use the tip of your round-nose pliers to form a simple loop that matches the size of the eye loop. Repeat 7 times. Repeat 6 times using dark gray pearls. Set the pearl links aside.

2 Trim 6 head pins to 1¾" (4.4 cm) each and set aside.

3 Attach the toggle ring to one 4mm jump ring. Attach the previous jump ring to one 6mm jump ring and 1 loop of 1 black pearl link.

4 Use one 6mm jump ring to attach 1 dark gray pearl link to the previous link. Repeat 4 times attaching 1 dark gray pearl link, 3 black pearl links, and 1 dark gray pearl link.

5 String 1 dark gray pearl onto a 1¾" (4.4 cm) head pin and form a simple loop at the top of the head pin. Attach the loop to the 6mm jump ring attached to the last black pearl link on the free end of the chain from Step 4.

6 String 1 dark gray pearl onto a 1¾" (4.4 cm) head pin and form a simple loop at the top of the head pin. Repeat 3 times. Use one 6mm jump ring to string the loop on 1 head pin and the shaft of the previous attached head pin. Repeat 3 times.

7 Cut the head off of one 1¾" (4.4 cm) head pin and form a simple loop on each end of the wire. Use one 6mm jump ring to attach 1 loop to the shaft of the previous attached head pin.

8 Connect three 4mm jump rings into a chain. Attach one end of the chain to the toggle bar and the opposite end to one 6mm jump ring. Attach the previous jump ring to 1 loop of 1 black pearl link from Step 1. Repeat Step 4.

9 Attach the free loop from Step 7 to the last 6mm jump ring from Step 8.

10 String 1 light gray pearl onto a 2" (5.1 cm) head pin and form a simple loop at the top of the head pin. Repeat 4 times.

11 Attach the loop on 1 light gray pearl head pin to the loop on the last dark gray pearl link on the left (toggle ring) side of the necklace.

12 Use one 6mm jump ring to string 1 loop on 1 light gray head pin and the shaft of the previous attached head pin. Repeat 3 times.

13 Cut the head off of a 2" (5.1 cm) head pin and form a simple loop on each end. Use one 6mm jump ring to attach 1 loop to the shaft of the previous attached head pin. Attach the other loop to the last dark gray pearl link on the right (toggle bar) side of the necklace.

Off the Cuff

Embellish a plain leather bracelet with crystal-and-raku-studded ring blanks for a corsage-style cuff suitable for an urban cowgirl.

TIP

Adding your links in order makes it easier to get all of the dangles onto the ring form.

MOLLY SCHALLER

Materials

- 10 light silk 6mm faceted-crystal rounds (A)
- 2 light silk 8mm faceted-crystal rounds (B)
- 7 topaz AB 8mm helix crystal rounds (C)
- 10 rust raku 4×9mm ceramic rondelles (D)
- 6 rust raku 10mm ceramic rounds (E)
- 4 topaz AB faceted 6×4mm crystal rondelles (F)
- 1 topaz AB faceted 8×6mm crystal rondelles (G)
- 1 brown 9×¾" (22.9×1.9 cm) leather cuff blank
- 3 copper 10-loop ring blanks
- 40 copper 2" (5 cm) head pins

Tools

Round-nose pliers
2 pairs of chain-nose pliers
Wire cutters
Ball-peen hammer
Bench block

Techniques *(see page 130)*

Simple loops

Finished Size

6½–8¼" (16.5–21 cm) adjustable

Variation

This version by Michelle Mach uses inexpensive pressed-glass rounds and flowers. Instead of pressing the rings tightly against the cuff, bend the rings into looser rectangular sliders. This allows you to slide the rings on and off to change the look.

1 Use your fingers and then the hammer and bench block to straighten all 3 ring blanks into a flat shape. Be careful not to damage the loops.

2 Use your fingers to form each ring blank into a "slider" that will go over the leather cuff. You may need to use chain-nose pliers to bend the corners and pinch the ring blank onto the cuff. Slide all 3 ring blanks onto the cuff.

3 Use 1 head pin to string 1 light silk 6mm faceted round. Trim the wire and make a simple loop. Repeat with the remaining beads to create a total of 40 dangles.

4 Position the bracelet cuff horizontally on your work surface with the clasp on the left. The ring blanks will all be positioned vertically on the cuff.

Note: Loops 1–5 are on the left side of each ring blank and loops 6–10 are on the right side of each ring blank.

5 Open the simple loop on each dangle and add them in the following order to the left ring blank: Loop 1: D; 2: C; 3: E, A; 4: C; 5: A; 6: A; 7: D, E; 8: C; 9: D, A; 10: A. Repeat this step for the right ring blank.

6 Add the following to the center ring blank: Loop 1: F, D; 2: E; 3: G; 4: D; 5: B, F; 6: B, F; 7: D; 8: C; 9: E; 10: F, D.

Queen of Thorns

Transform cones into spikes and use soldered jump rings for smooth spacers in this dramatic necklace studded with silky pearls, sparkling glass rounds, and rough lava beads.

TIP

Wrap the tips of your chain- or flat-nose pliers with painter's tape to prevent scratching glass pearls or plated metals.

ANDREW THORNTON

Materials

- 1 red magma 30mm crystal navette pendant
- 14 fuchsia 12mm 2-way faceted-glass coins
- 6 burgundy 10mm glass pearls
- 8 burgundy 8mm glass pearls
- 18 burgundy 6mm glass pearls
- 18 black 10mm lava rounds
- 10 metallic gold iris Japanese size 8° seed beads
- 8 gunmetal-plated 9×21mm cones
- 8 antique copper 22-gauge 3" (7.6 cm) ball-end head pins
- 1 copper 18-gauge 8mm jump ring
- 14 antique copper 18-gauge 8mm soldered jump rings
- 2 copper 2×3mm crimp tubes
- 1 copper 20mm toggle clasp
- 23" (58.4 cm) of gold .019 flexible beading wire

Tools

Round-nose pliers
2 pairs of chain- or flat-nose pliers
Crimping pliers
Wire cutters

Techniques *(see page 130)*

Crimping ▪ Jump rings ▪ Stringing ▪ Wrapped loops

Finished Size

21½" (54.6 cm)

Variation

Play with cones of varying widths and lengths to change the feeling of the necklace from stubby, lethal spikes to delicate, icicle-like drops.

1 Use 1 head pin to string 1 seed bead, the small end of 1 cone, and one 8mm pearl. Form a wrapped loop and trim the excess wire. Repeat this entire step 7 times. Set aside.

2 Use the 8mm copper jump ring to string the crystal pendant; close the jump ring. Set aside.

3 Use the flexible beading wire to string 1 crimp tube, 1 seed bead, and one half of the toggle clasp. Pass the wire back through the seed bead and tube and crimp the tube with crimping pliers. Trim the excess wire.

4 String one 10mm pearl. String 1 lava round, 1 soldered jump ring, 1 lava round, 1 soldered jump ring, 1 lava round, and 1 glass coin; repeat. String 1 lava round, 1 soldered jump ring, 1 lava round, 1 soldered jump ring, 1 lava round, and one 10mm pearl.

5 String 1 glass coin, one 6mm pearl, 1 cone dangle, and one 6mm glass pearl; repeat 3 times. String 1 glass coin, 1 soldered jump ring, one 10mm pearl, and one 6mm pearl.

6 String the pendant and repeat Steps 5 and 4 in reverse order for the other half of the necklace.

7 String 1 crimp tube, 1 seed bead, and the remaining half of the toggle clasp. Pass the wire back through the seed bead and tube. Crimp the tube with crimping pliers. Trim the excess wire.

I Dream of the Sea

Spiral fancy head pins into sea green circles and bright silver curves that echo the rolling waves of the sea.

ERIN PRAIS-HINTZ

Materials

- 1 yellow/teal/blue polymer clay 24×38mm oval "Dream" focal connector
- 24 white 5–10mm branch coral chips (A)
- 5 mother-of-pearl 15mm shell drop discs
- 2 green 8–12×12–16mm everlasting small side-cut seashells
- 5 assorted 5–11×9–14mm pink/white seashells
- 1 nautilus 18×15mm spiral shell
- 14 opaque turquoise Picasso-finish 6.8×9mm fire-polished glass rondelles (B)
- 12 clear turquoise Picasso-finish 9.7×13.5mm fire-polished glass beads (C)
- 3 assorted polymer clay 11.5mm rondelles
- 69 sea green swirl matte 2×4mm peanut beads
- 2 turquoise polymer clay 17.5mm round disc **head pins**
- 1 yellow polymer clay 17.5mm round disc **head pin**
- 11 silver-plated 2" (5.1 cm) fancy star ball-end **head pins**
- 21 silver-plated 4mm daisy spacers (D)
- 4 silver-plated 5mm jump rings
- 5 silver-plated 6mm jump rings
- 2 silver-plated 8mm jump rings
- 2 silver 2mm crimp tubes
- 1 pewter 22mm starfish toggle clasp
- 14" (35.6 cm) of .015 flexible beading wire

Tools

Round-nose pliers
2 pairs of chain-nose pliers
Crimping pliers
Wire cutters
Chasing hammer
Bench block
11.5 and 7mm pen or dowel
Bead stops (optional)

Techniques *(see page 130)*

Crimping ▪ Hammering ▪ Jump rings
▪ Spirals ▪ Stringing ▪ Wrapped
loops (variation)

Finished Size

18" (45.7 cm)

Variation

Mimic the look of fancy head pins by stringing tiny bead caps or flower beads on the ends of ball-end head pins.

"Beginning jewelry makers often don't take their time and growing talents into account when pricing their work. Your vision is worth every penny you charge."
—Erin Prais-Hintz

1 Using a pen or a dowel as a mandrel, make an 11.5mm loop at the top of the turquoise polymer disc on 1 polymer disc head pin. Wrap the excess wire around the base, leaving a ¾" (2 cm) tail. Bring the tail to the front of the disc and use the tip of your round-nose pliers to make a small tight spiral. Hammer the top of the loop to flatten and work-harden it, taking care not to damage the polymer disc. Repeat this entire step with the yellow polymer clay disc head pin.

2 Repeat Step 1 with the remaining turquoise polymer disc head pin except make a 7mm loop at the top of the polymer disc and turn the loop so it is perpendicular to the disc. Set aside.

3 String 14 peanut beads on 1 star head pin. Gently curve the head pin into a circle. String the beaded head pin circle through the 11.5mm loop on the turquoise polymer disc head pin from Step 1. Wrap the tail of the beaded head pin around the base to secure. Trim any excess wire and tuck in the end securely.

4 Create a second beaded head pin circle and string it through the 11.5mm loop on the yellow polymer disc head pin and the 11.5mm loop on the previous polymer disc head pin before completing the wrap. Create a third beaded head pin circle and connect it to the 11.5mm loop on the yellow polymer disc head pin.

5 Create a fourth beaded head pin circle and use one 8mm jump ring to connect it to the previous beaded head pin circle.

6 Connect one 6mm jump ring to the last beaded head pin circle added. Use one 5mm jump ring to connect the starfish toggle ring to the previous jump ring.

7 Connect one 6mm jump ring the first beaded head pin circle on the opposite end. Use one 8mm jump ring to connect the polymer clay focal connector to the previous jump ring.

8 Mix the seashells together. Use 1 star head pin to string 1 seashell. Place your round-nose pliers at the top of the seashell and begin a wrapped loop but do not wrap it. Repeat 6 times for a total of 7 seashell dangles. Set 1 dangle aside.

9 Connect 1 seashell dangle to the 6mm jump ring in Step 7, complete the wrap 2–3 times, and form a tight spiral with the tail as in Step 1. Repeat this step to attach 2 seashell dangles to the 11.5mm loop on the turquoise polymer disc head pin, 2 seashell dangles to the 11.5mm loop on the yellow polymer disc head pin, and 1 seashell dangle to the 8mm jump ring in Step 6.

10 Use one 6mm jump ring to attach 1 shell disc to the 6mm jump ring in Step 7, each 11.5mm loop in Step 9, and the 8mm jump ring in Step 5.

11 Use the beading wire to string 1 crimp tube, 5 peanut beads, the turquoise polymer disc head pin from Step 2, the free hole in the polymer focal connector, and 5 peanut beads. Pass the wire back through the crimp tube and crimp with crimping pliers, taking care not to break the glass peanut beads.

12 String the following: 1 shell disc (with 6mm jump ring), 1 nautilus shell, the remaining seashell dangle from Step 7, 3A, 1 polymer rondelle, 3A, 1 polymer rondelle, 3A, 1 polymer rondelle, 3A, 1C, 3A, 1C, 3A, 1C, 1D, 1B, 1D, 1C, 1D, 1B, 1D, 1C, 1D, 1C. String 1D and 1B ten times. String 1D, 1C, 1D, 1C, 1D, 1B, 1D, 1C, 1D, 1B, 1D, 1C, 3A, 1C, 3A, 1C, 3 peanut beads, 1 crimp tube, and the toggle bar. Pass the wire back through the tube and crimp. Trim the excess wire.

Metal Mixology

Alternating brass and copper cones creates a sleek metal bracelet cuff that works equally well for men or women.

TIP
To change the size of this bracelet, calculate about 6 cones per 1" (2.5 cm).

MICHELLE MACH

Materials

- 4 copper 4mm rounds
- 18 copper 5×12mm cones
- 17 brass 5×12mm cones
- 2 brass 2" (5.1 cm) eye pins
- 1 copper 5mm jump ring
- 1 brass 4mm jump ring
- 1 brass 5×20mm hammered teardrop toggle clasp
- 4' (1.2 m) of black .006 thermally bonded beading thread
- 2" (5.1 cm) of copper 2×4mm oval chain

Tools

Round-nose pliers
2 pairs of chain- or flat-nose pliers
Wire cutters
Scissors
Beading needle (optional)

Techniques *(see page 130)*

Jump rings ▪ Ladder stitch ▪ Simple loops ▪ Square knot

Finished Size

7" (17.8 cm)

Variation

Substitute a slide-lock clasp for the toggle clasp to give this bracelet a tighter fit.

1 Use the thread to string 1 copper cone (small to large end) and 1 brass cone (small to large end). Repeat the thread path several times, making sure the long sides of the cones are flush against one another. End with the thread exiting the large end of the brass cone.

2 String 1 copper cone (small to large end) and pass back through the previous brass cone and back through the copper cone just strung. Repeat this entire step attaching alternating copper and brass cones. Form a square knot, using the tip of your round-nose pliers to help place the knot deep inside the last copper cone. Trim.

3 Use 1 eye pin to string the small end of 1 copper cone on one end of the woven strand. String 2 copper rounds inside the large end of the cone and form a simple loop. Attach one end of 1" (2.5 cm) of chain to 1 simple loop. Attach the other end of the chain to the other simple loop. Use 1 copper jump ring to attach the ring half of the clasp to the center chain link. Repeat this entire step at the other end of the woven strand using the remaining 1" (2.5 cm) of chain, the brass jump ring, and the bar half of the clasp.

Downtown Arts District

Make your own wire S-clasps and link them to form a beautiful, handmade chain that highlights your favorite art beads from galleries and artist enclaves.

TIP

Making your own clasps allows you to choose the exact metal and size you want, but using commercially made clasps speeds up the design process. If you do not make your own S-clasps, substitute 12 sterling silver ⅞" (cm) S-clasps for the 16-gauge sterling silver wire.

CINDY WIMMER

Materials

- 7 assorted 15×15mm lampwork-glass rounds
- 6 Thai hill tribe silver 4×4mm 3-sided stamped spacers
- 14 sterling silver 3×12mm bead caps
- 22 sterling silver 18-gauge 6.5×5mm oval jump rings
- 3 sterling silver 16-gauge 9mm round jump rings
- 2 sterling silver 3.5mm crimp covers
- 2 sterling silver 2mm crimp tubes
- 36" (91.4 cm) of 16-gauge sterling silver wire (for S-clasps)
- 10" (25.4 cm) of .019 flexible beading wire

Tools

Round-nose pliers
2 pairs of chain- or flat-nose pliers
Crimping pliers
Stepped pliers or 7mm mandrel
Flush cutters
Flat file
Chasing hammer
Rawhide or plastic mallet
Bench block
Liver of sulfur gel (optional)
Fine steel wool (#0000; optional)
Polishing cloth (optional)
Rotary tumbler (optional)
Mixed stainless-steel shot (optional)

Techniques *(see page 130)*

Crimp covers ▪ Crimping ▪ Jump rings ▪ Stringing ▪ Oxidizing (optional) ▪ Tumbling (optional)

Finished Size

17¾" (45.1 cm)

S-CLASPS

1 Flush cut and file the ends of a 2 ⅞" (7.3 cm) piece of silver wire. Grasp one end of the wire with the tip of your round-nose pliers. Roll the wire forward to create a simple loop. Repeat, creating another simple loop on the other end of the wire facing the opposite direction.

2 Grasp the wire with the 7mm barrel of the stepped pliers just under the loop, with the loop facing you. Roll the wire forward until it forms a hook shape. Repeat on the opposite end of the wire.

3 Close both hook ends to use the clasp as a link. Hammer the clasp on the bench block with the rawhide mallet to work-harden and then flatten the curves on both ends with a chasing hammer. Repeat Steps 1–3 eleven times for a total of 12 S-clasps.

NECKLACE

1 If desired, oxidize the S-clasps, jump rings, bead caps, crimp covers, and silver spacers with liver of sulfur. Rinse and dry. Place the components in a rotary tumbler with mixed stainless-steel shot to polish and work-harden or add shine with a polishing cloth.

2 To create 1 chain, connect 1 S-clasp to another with 2 oval jump rings. Use 2 oval jump rings to connect the previous S-clasp to another S-clasp. Repeat 3 times to create a chain of 6-clasps and 10 jump rings. Repeat this entire step to create a second chain.

3 Use the flexible beading wire to string 1 crimp tube and the S-clasp on one end of 1 chain. Pass the wire back through the tube and crimp the tube with crimping pliers. Trim the flexible beading wire.

4 String {1 bead cap, 1 lampwork-glass round, 1 bead cap, and 1 silver spacer} 6 times. String 1 bead cap, 1 lampwork-glass round, 1 bead cap, 1 crimp tube, and one end of the second chain. Pass the wire back through the tube and crimp. Trim the flexible beading wire. Cover the tubes with crimp covers.

5 Open the final hook on the end of 1 chain slightly. Open one 9mm jump ring and attach it to 2 more 9mm jump rings, forming an extension chain. Attach one end of the extension chain to the free end of the second chain with a pair of oval jump rings.

Variation

Make a two-tone variation by using an alternative metal for the bead caps and jump rings. You can also make a bracelet chain with the S-clasps and hang smaller lampwork beads, or any favorite beads, as charm dangles.

Mademoiselle Fleur

At first glance, this sweet pearl bracelet appears to feature a large copper filigree flower. Upon close inspection you might notice that the flower is made of several bead caps linked with jump rings.

TIP

Crystal pearls feature uniform holes that fit the eye pins perfectly. If you opt for freshwater pearls, you may need to use a bead reamer to make the holes uniform or make a strung design instead of using beaded links. Using wire above 22g is not recommended, as the softer wire links will be easily bent when worn.

MICHELLE MACH

Materials

- 1 hunter green 10mm crystal pearl
- 2 deep brown 8mm crystal pearls
- 2 brown 7mm crystal pearls
- 4 bronze 6mm crystal pearls
- 1 brass 60×22mm diamond filigree connector
- 6 copper 10mm filigree bead caps
- 1 brass 3" (7.6 cm) 24-gauge head pin
- 8 brass 21-gauge 1" eye pins
- 3 copper 4mm jump rings
- 3 copper 8mm jump rings
- 4 brass 7.5mm jump rings
- 12 brass 4mm jump rings
- 2 brass 10mm etched jump rings
- 1 brass 19.5×7mm marquis filigree pearl clasp

Tools

Round-nose pliers
2 pairs of chain- or flat-nose pliers
Wire cutters
6mm/8.5mm bail-making pliers
(optional)

Techniques *(see page 130)*

Filigree forming ▪ Jump rings ▪ Simple
loops ▪ Wire wrapping

Finished Size

7½" (19.1 cm)

Variation

Create a whimsical flower pendant with gold-plated filigree bead caps, a peridot glass rondelle, a tiny gold bead cap, a handmade green-and-ivory ceramic round, and a pair of brass leaves attached to a hidden brass gear. Complete the necklace with a touch of green glass and delicate gold-plated chain.

1 Use bail-making pliers or your hands to gently bend the filigree connector into a slight arc. Set aside.

2 Use one 8mm copper jump ring to attach the center holes of 2 bead caps. Repeat twice to create 3 bead-cap pairs. Use one 4mm copper jump ring to connect each 8mm jump ring together beneath the bead-cap petals, creating a circle.

3 Use the head pin to string 1 copper round, the green pearl, the center of the bead-cap circle, and the center hole of the filigree connector. Use the tail end of the head pin to weave across the back of the filigree connector, up through the top (under the bead-cap petals), and across the back. Tuck in the wire end. Use two 7.5mm jump rings to attach 1 etched jump ring to the 2 holes on one end of the filigree connector; repeat on the other end.

4 Use 1 eye pin to string 1 deep brown pearl; form a simple loop. Repeat. Use 1 eye pin to string 1 brown pearl; form a simple loop. Repeat. Use 1 eye pin to string 1 bronze pearl; form a simple loop. Repeat 3 times. Set the pearl links aside.

5 Use two 4mm jump rings to attach the etched jump ring from Step 3 to 1 deep brown pearl link. Use one 4mm jump ring to attach the previous link to 1 brown pearl link. Use one 4mm jump ring to attach the previous link to 1 bronze pearl link. Use one 4mm jump ring to attach another bronze pearl link. Use one 4mm jump ring to attach the previous link to half of the clasp. Repeat this entire step for the other half of the bracelet.

Silver Lining

Flower-shaped bead caps make darling umbrella dangles that can be changed on a whim using spring-ring clasps. Connect the aluminum clouds with head pins to hold extra raindrops.

Materials

- 12 Montana blue 4×6mm glass teardrops
- 86 clear 4×3mm glass teardrops
- 21 copper metal size 11° metal seed beads
- 2 copper-plated 5mm rope spacers
- 1 copper-plated 6mm daisy spacer
- 2 pewter 5mm daisy spacers
- 3 aluminum 27×22mm cloud blanks
- 1 copper 17×7mm flower **bead cap**
- 1 brown 18×6mm enameled flower **bead cap**
- 1 melon 20×8mm porcelain flower **bead cap**
- 2 silver-plated 2" (5.1 cm) **head pins**
- 73 silver-plated 4mm jump rings
- 5 silver-plated 5mm jump rings
- 1 silver-plated 12×4mm barrel clasp
- 3 silver-plated 6mm **spring-ring clasps**
- 2½" (6.4 cm) of silver 20-gauge craft wire
- 6" (15.2 cm) of silver 26-gauge craft wire
- 5" (12.7 cm) of bronze 20-gauge craft wire
- 5" (12.7 cm) of bronze 24-gauge craft wire
- 3" (7.6 cm) of bronze 26-gauge craft wire
- 19" (48.3 cm) of antiqued silver-plated 11×1mm curved bar chain

Tools

Round-nose pliers
2 pairs of chain- or flat-nosed pliers
Wire cutters
1.8mm metal hole-punch pliers
Permanent marker
Texturing or ball-peen hammer (optional)
Metal design stamp (optional)
Bench block (optional)

Techniques (see page 130)

Coiling ▪ Hole punching ▪ Jump rings
Simple loops ▪ Spirals ▪ Hammering
(optional) ▪ Metal stamping (optional)

Finished Size

22" (55.9 cm)

MICHELLE MACH

Variation

Hang clear teardrops along the edges of a silver-colored filigree bead cap or use colored craft wire for extra drama as shown with the red-and-black umbrella. Smaller bead caps (8–10mm) make sweet earrings.

Tip

Sometimes hole punches can leave light scratches or marks. For the prettiest results, punch the holes in the clouds on the back side of the blanks.

1 Arrange the 3 cloud blanks next to one another horizontally, slightly overlapping them. Use a marker to mark the places to punch holes. Punch 3 holes in first cloud: upper left, bottom left, and middle right. Punch 5 holes in middle cloud: upper left (overlapping with middle right hole on first cloud), 3 holes on the bottom, and 1 hole middle right. Punch 3 holes in the last cloud: upper left (overlapping with the middle right on the previous cloud), bottom middle, and middle right. If desired, use the texturing hammer, ball-peen hammer, and metal design stamps to add texture.

2 Use 1 head pin to string the overlapping holes on the first 2 clouds. Form a simple loop. Repeat with the middle and last cloud.

3 Cut the chain in half. Use one 4mm jump ring to attach half of the clasp to one end of 1 chain. Use one 4mm jump ring to attach the other end of this chain to the left hole on the first cloud. Repeat for other half of the necklace, using the other half of the clasp and the right hole on the last cloud.

4 Use one 4mm jump ring to string 1–3 clear teardrops. Repeat 34 times. Attach each jump ring to the ring in between 2 bar links on the chain. Use one 4mm jump ring to string 1 Montana blue teardrop. Repeat 11 times. Attach the Montana blue teardrops randomly to the chain. Attach additional clear teardrops/jump rings to the jump rings already attached to the chain.

5 Use one 4mm jump ring to string 1–3 clear teardrops and then attach the jump ring to 1 simple loop on 1 cloud. Repeat. Use one 4mm jump ring to string 1–3 clear teardrops. Repeat 8 times. Use one 5mm jump ring to attach 1 teardrop dangle to the 5 bottom holes in the clouds. Attach the remaining 3 teardrop dangles randomly to the previous 4mm jump rings.

6 Use 2½" (6.4 cm) of silver 20g craft wire to form a simple loop. String 1 pewter daisy spacer, 1 copper bead cap, and 1 pewter daisy spacer. Form a spiral at the end of the wire. Use the 26g silver craft wire to form a tight coil around the 20g wire. Trim the tails and pinch in the ends with chain-nose pliers. Wrap the 26g bronze craft wire loosely around the silver coil. Trim the excess wire and pinch in the tail ends. Attach 1 spring-ring clasp to the simple loop on the umbrella. Use 2½" (6.4 cm) of bronze 20g craft wire to form a simple loop. String 1 copper-plated daisy spacer and 1 brown bead cap. Form a curl at the end of the wire. Using the 24g bronze craft wire, coil 3–5 times around the 20g bronze craft wire and then leave a ⅛" (3.2 mm) gap, repeat until the end of the 20g wire. Attach 1 spring-ring clasp to the simple loop on the umbrella. Use 2½" (6.4 cm) of 20g bronze craft wire to form a simple loop. String 1 rope spacer, 1 melon bead cap, and 1 rope spacer. String 21 copper seed beads. Form a curve at the end of the wire and then form a simple loop on the tail. Attach 1 spring-ring clasp to the simple loop on the umbrella.

7 Use the spring-ring clasps to attach 1 umbrella to the bottom of each cloud.

Fiesta

Use knot cups to make quick-
and-easy silk-tassel dangles
for a casual necklace to wear
at your next weekend get-
together with friends.

TIP
You can use
chain-nose pliers
or crimping
pliers to close
knot cups.

ERIN SIEGEL

Materials

- 24 chartreuse 6mm pressed-glass rounds
- 24 silver-plated 4×6mm knot cups
- 32 silver-plated 5mm jump rings
- 2 silver-plated 4×12mm foldover cord ends
- 1 silver-plated 9mm spring-ring clasp
- 36" (91.4 cm) of tan 3/16" (4.8 mm) deerskin leather lace
- 1 card of amethyst size 12 silk knotting cord with attached needle
- 1 card of coral size 12 silk knotting cord with attached needle
- 1 card of emerald size 12 silk knotting cord with attached needle
- 1 card of bright yellow size 12 silk knotting cord with attached needle
- Fabric cement (optional)

Tools

2 pairs of chain-nose pliers
1/16" (1.6 mm) leather hole punch
Scissors
Ruler
Pen

Techniques *(see page 130)*

Double overhand knot ■ Foldover cord ends ■ Hole punching ■ Jump rings ■ Knot cups ■ Overhand knots ■ Stringing ■ Gluing (optional) ■ Knotting with tweezers

Finished Size

35½" (90.2 cm) adjustable to 36½" (92.7 cm)

Variation

String several black-and-silver tassels on choker-length gunmetal chain for an edgier look.

1 Remove all the cord from 1 card. Tie a double overhand knot at the end of the cord opposite the needle. Trim. Dab the knot with glue if desired. Let dry. String 1 knot cup and close it. Tie an overhand knot. String 1 chartreuse round and form an overhand knot. Trim the cord to ½" (1.3 cm) from the last knot and fray the ends. Repeat 5 more times.

2 Repeat Step 1 for the rest of the carded silk cord colors for a total of 24 tassel dangles, 6 in each color of cord. Set aside.

3 Insert the leather lace into 1 foldover end and close it with chain-nose pliers. Attach the spring-ring clasp to the loop of the foldover end.

4 Lay the leather lace on the ruler. Use the pen to mark the center of the leather ¾" (1.9 cm) from the end of the foldover finding. Mark the remaining leather every 1½" (3.8 cm). Punch holes through all the marked places in the leather with the leather hole punch.

5 Use 1 jump ring to string 1 coral tassel dangle and attach it to the first hole in the leather lace. Repeat using 1 purple tassel in the second hole, 1 yellow tassel in the third hole, and 1 green tassel in the fourth hole. Repeat this sequence 5 times, except set the final green tassel aside.

6 Insert the free end of the leather lace into 1 foldover end and close. Connect 9 jump rings together to create a chain extension. Attach one end of the chain to the loop of the foldover end and attach the final green tassel to the opposite end.

Searching for Simplicity

Turn two copper bails upside down to join smooth light green glass rounds to faceted dark red glass rondelles in perfect harmony.

TIP
Use a drop of superglue to keep cones from moving and to hide closed crimp tubes.

ANDREW THORNTON

Materials

- 1 terra-cotta 27mm polymer clay pendant
- 16 Picasso-finish brick 8×6mm fire-polished glass rondelles
- 6 aqua-and-gold 8mm fire-polished glass rounds
- 24 spring green 8mm cultured sea-glass rounds
- 20 copper size 6° metal seed beads
- 80 (about 1 gram) chartreuse silver-lined size 11° Japanese seed beads
- 2 copper-plated 6×12mm **bails**
- 2 copper-plated 11×9mm cones
- 6 copper 2" (5.1 cm) rose-colored ball-end head pins
- 4 copper 3mm crimp covers
- 6 copper 2×3mm crimp tubes
- 1 copper-plated 15×20mm toggle clasp
- 23" (58.4 cm) of gold .019 flexible beading wire
- Superglue

Tools

Round-nose pliers
Chain- or flat-nose pliers
Crimping pliers
Wire cutters

Techniques *(see page 130)*

Crimp covers ▪ Crimping ▪ Stringing ▪ Wrapped loops

Finished Size

19" (48.3 cm)

Variation

Hang multiple beaded loops from each bail for a fuller-looking necklace.

"Keep making work and challenging yourself. An Olympic athlete is not expected to win a gold medal by dumb luck; you have to build and stretch your creative muscles by making something every day."
—Andrew Thornton

1 Use 1 head pin to string 1 aqua-and-gold round; form a wrapped loop. Repeat 5 times.

2 Use 10" (25.4 cm) of flexible beading wire to string 1 crimp tube, 40 chartreuse seed beads, and the tube of the bail. Pass the wire back through the crimp tube and crimp.

3 String the small end of 1 cone. Glue the tip of the cone to secure. Let dry.

4 String 2 rondelles and 1 dangle from Step 1; repeat 2 times. String 2 rondelles.

5 String the pendant. Repeat Step 4. String the large end of the remaining cone, 1 crimp tube, 40 chartreuse seed beads, and the tube of the second bail. Pass the wire back through the crimp tube and the cone and snug the beads. Crimp the tube and tuck it into the top of the cone. Glue the tip of the cone to secure. Let dry. Trim the excess wire.

6 Use 6½" (16.5 cm) of flexible beading wire to string 1 crimp tube, 1 glass round, and the loop of 1 bail. Pass the wire back through bead and tube and crimp. Cover the crimp with a crimp cover. String 1 glass round and 1 copper seed bead; repeat 8 times. String 1 glass round, 1 crimp tube, 1 glass round, 1 copper seed bead, and one half of the toggle clasp. Pass the wire back through the glass round, the crimp tube, and the glass round. Crimp the tube and trim the excess wire. Cover the tube with a crimp cover. Repeat this entire step for other side of the necklace.

Owl at the Moon

Open bead frames connected with
ball-end head pins make window-
like openings especially fitting for
a tree house–inspired necklace,
complete with a cute owl and
a leafy branch.

TIP

If you can't find
vintage beaded chain,
you can make your own
chain by creating beaded
links with eye pins and
either connecting them
directly to one another
or using jump rings
in between the links.

LORELEI EURTO

Materials

- 1 polymer clay 25×35mm owl pendant
- 5 green glass 12×16mm leaves
- 1 brown/magenta/orange ceramic 20mm Kazuri bull's-eye coin
- 13 copper 10mm etched coins
- 6 ruby jade 5×10mm faceted rondelles
- 7 silver-plated 18mm bead frames
- 20 copper 2" (5.1 cm) ball-end head pins
- 7 copper 6mm jump rings
- 3 copper 4mm jump rings
- 2 copper 2mm crimp tubes
- 1 copper 15×20mm toggle clasp
- 3" (7.6 cm) of copper 18-gauge wire
- 3" (7.6 cm) of .019 flexible beading wire
- 9" (22.9 cm) of green vintage Lucite 4mm beaded chain
- Liver of sulfur (optional)

Tools

Round-nose pliers
2 pairs of flat-nose pliers
Wire cutters
Ball-peen hammer (optional)
Bench block (optional)
Fine steel wool (#0000; optional)

Techniques *(see page 130)*

Crimping ■ Jump rings ■ Stringing ■ Wrapped loops ■ Hammering (optional) ■ Oxidizing (optional)

Finished Size

22" (55.8 cm)

Wire wrap the outside of the bead frames with tiny glass leaves or flowers to play up the tree-house theme.

1 If desired, use the ball end of the hammer to texture the bead frames on the bench block. Use a liver of sulfur solution to darken the frames. Rinse and dry. Remove the excess patina with fine steel wool. Set aside.

2 Use one 6mm copper jump ring to attach the owl pendant to the toggle ring.

3 Attach one 4mm copper jump ring to the loop on the toggle ring but don't close the jump ring. Separate the beaded chain into two 4½" (11.4 cm) lengths with 2 pairs of chain- or flat-nose pliers. Attach one end of each beaded chain to the 4mm jump ring; close the jump ring.

4 Begin a wrapped loop on one end of the 3" (7.6 cm) copper wire. Attach the free end of each beaded chain to the loop and complete the wrap. String the Kazuri bead and begin a second wrapped loop but don't wrap it yet.

5 Using 1 head pin, string 1 hole in the bead frame from the inside going out. String 1 copper coin bead and form a wrapped loop. Repeat on the other side of the bead frame. Repeat this entire step to create a total of 6 beaded frame links. String 1 head pin through 1 hole in the remaining bead frame. String 1 copper coin bead, and form a wrapped loop.

6 Connect the links together with six 6mm jump rings. Attach the wrapped loop on the end of the beaded frame link chain to the open loop on the Kazuri bead from Step 4. Complete that wire-wrapped loop.

7 Use 1 head pin to string 1 jade rondelle and form a wrapped loop. Repeat 5 times. Attach 1 dangle to each 6mm jump ring from Step 6. Using 1 head pin, string the free hole in the last bead frame from the inside going out; form a wrapped loop.

8 String 1 crimp tube onto one end of the flexible beading wire. String the wire through the end wrapped loop in Step 7. Pass the wire back through the crimp tube and flatten using flat-nose pliers. String 5 glass leaf beads, 1 crimp tube, and one 4mm jump ring. Pass the wire back through the crimp tube and flatten. Attach another 4mm jump ring to the toggle bar and to the previous 4mm jump ring.

Vintage Revival

In this lush necklace, pin converters turn a vintage brooch into a pendant, secure multiple strands of pearls, and form a unique clasp.

TIP

If you don't have a treasured brooch stashed in your jewelry box, find one at an antique mall, garage sale, or online.

TIP

If using a horizontal pin converter, test your brooch to be sure it's not top heavy. If the brooch flops forward when worn as a pendant, try a vertical pin converter or one with a longer tube instead.

CINDY WIMMER

Materials

- 1 vintage 40×54mm brooch
- 6 gold-and-crystal 6×2mm rondelles
- 1 crystal AB 10mm round
- 50 white 7×8mm nugget pearls
- 71 rose champagne 5×4mm rice pearls
- 1 gold-plated 30.5×9.5mm vertical pin converter
- 2 gold-plated 21×13.5 horizontal **pin converters**
- 4 gold-plated 2mm crimp tubes
- 1 matte gold 22mm lobster clasp
- 4" (10.2 cm) of 18-gauge red brass wire
- 3" (7.6 cm) of 20-gauge red brass wire
- 37" (94 cm) of .015 gold satin flexible beading wire
- 15½" (39.4 cm) of gold-plated unsoldered rolo chain

Tools

Round-nose pliers
Chain-nose pliers
Flat-nose pliers
Crimping pliers
Wire cutters

Techniques *(see page 130)*

Crimping ▪ Simple loops ▪ Stringing ▪ Wrapped loops

Finished Size

17¼" (43.8 cm)

Variation

Add as many strands as you like, making the simple loop larger to accommodate the strands. If the strands are heavier, be sure to use thicker-gauge wire, such as 16g.

1 Slide the vertical pin converter onto the open pin of the vintage brooch. Close the pin and set it aside.

2 Cut the 18g red brass wire into two 2" (5.1 cm) pieces. Use the tip of your round-nose pliers to form a simple loop on one end of 1 piece of wire. Insert this wire through the tube of 1 horizontal pin converter and trim the tail wire to ⅜" (9.5 mm); make a second simple loop. Repeat with the remaining horizontal pin converter; set aside.

3 Use 3" (7.6 cm) of 20g red brass wire to form a wrapped loop that attaches to the teardrop loop on 1 horizontal pin converter. String the crystal round; form a wrapped loop that attaches to the lobster clasp. Open the last link on one end of the chain and attach it to the top simple loop on the previous horizontal pin converter. Open the last link on the other end of the chain and attach it to the top simple loop on the other horizontal pin converter.

4 Use 18" (45.7 cm) of flexible beading wire to string 1 crimp tube and the top simple loop of 1 horizontal pin converter just below the chain. Pass the wire back through the tube and crimp the tube with crimping pliers. String all the rice pearls, 1 crimp tube, and the top simple loop of the other horizontal pin converter, again below the chain. Pass the wire back through the tube and crimp. Trim the flexible beading wire.

5 Use 19" (48.3 cm) of flexible beading wire to string 1 crimp tube and the bottom simple loop on 1 horizontal pin converter. Pass the wire back through the tube and crimp. String 16 nugget pearls. String {1 rondelle and 3 nugget pearls} 3 times and the bail on the vertical pin converter (with the brooch attached). String {3 nugget pearls and 1 rondelle} 3 times, 16 nugget pearls, 1 crimp tube, and the bottom simple loop on the other horizontal pin converter. Pass the wire back through the tube and crimp. Trim the flexible beading wire.

Basic Techniques

While the number of techniques described here might seem daunting, keep in mind that most projects in this book rely on just five basic jewelry-making techniques: stringing, crimping, simple loops, jump rings, and wrapped loops. Some projects require additional skills, such as knotting or braiding, while others recommend, but do not require, optional finishing techniques, such as hammering or oxidizing. With this handy guide, you'll be ready for anything!

BEADWEAVING

ladder stitch

String 2 beads. Pass through them again. Add 1 bead and pass through the previous bead and the one just added. Repeat the figure-eight pattern, adding 1 bead at a time, until the ladder-stitched chain reaches the desired length.

STRINGING

stringing

Use wire, cord, or thread to pick up and gather beads on the strand.

CRIMPING

Crimp tubes: Use flexible beading wire to string 1 crimp tube and half of the clasp. Pass the wire back through the crimp tube, leaving a short (¼" or 6.4 mm) tail. Place the crimp tube in the back notches of the pliers, making sure the wires are parallel. Squeeze the pliers, securing each wire in its own chamber and compressing the tube into a U shape. Rotate the crimp tube 90° and place it in the front notch of the pliers.

Squeeze the pliers to fold the crimp in half so both chambers are on top of each other. Trim any excess wire.

Crimp beads: If using crimp beads, use chain- or flat-nose pliers to flatten the crimp.

using crimp covers

Position the crimp cover over the crimped tube. Use the front notch of the crimping pliers to gently close the crimp cover to create a round bead-like appearance.

using wire guards

Use flexible beading wire to string 1 crimp tube and the 1 tube (the first half) on 1 wire guard. String one half of the clasp, the second tube on the wire guard, and back through the crimp tube. Snug the crimp tube close to the wire guard and crimp.

KNOTTING AND WORKING WITH CORD AND RIBBON

making overhand knots

Use 1 cord to make a loop with the cord ends crossed. Pass one end of the cord through the middle of the loop and tighten.

making a double overhand knot

Create an overhand knot. Pass the cord through the loop a second time before tightening.

making slipknots

Fold the cord back onto itself. Use the short end to make a loop around the folded cord. Bring the cord behind and through the loop. Tighten.

making square knots

Form an overhand knot. Form a second overhand knot in the opposite direction.

using knot cups

String the hole of the knot cup. Form a knot at the end of the cord and place it inside the rounded cup. Use the front notch of your crimping pliers to close the cup.

knotting with tweezers

Make a loose overhand knot. Use the tweezers to move the knot to the desired location on the cord. Tighten the knot and remove the tweezers.

making a lark's head knot

Fold the thread, cord, or ribbon in half and use the folded end to string a jump ring, ring, or loop. Pull both ends of the cord through the strand loop.

braiding

Use 3 cords to form a loose overhand knot. Attach the knot to a macramé board or clipboard. Move the left cord between the middle and right cord. Move the right cord between the middle and left cord. Repeat until the braid reaches the desired length. Undo the overhand knot.

using crimp cord ends

Insert the cord into the crimp cord end and flatten with chain-nose pliers. If desired, dab glue inside the cord end before flattening.

using foldover cord ends

Place the end of the cord inside the middle section of a foldover cord end. Use your chain- or flat-nose pliers to bend the left and then the right sides of the cord end closed. If desired, you may add a drop of glue before closing the cord end.

gluing

Use a toothpick to dab glue where needed. If necessary, clamp or weight the item to help secure the connection. To glue very smooth items together, first roughen them with steel wool or sandpaper.

using ribbon ends

Place one end of ribbon inside the ribbon end. Use nylon-jaw or flat-nose pliers to close. If desired, place a drop of glue inside the ribbon end before closing.

METALWORK

forming

Use bail-making pliers to curve a metal or filigree component into the shape needed. Filigree is delicate; if you bend it back and forth too many times it will break. For thin (24- to 26-gauge) metal, you can use your flat-nose pliers to create more angular shapes. Sometimes the filigree is malleable enough to simply use your fingers to shape it.

filing

Move the metal file against the rough edge of metal in a repeated motion away from you. Always file in the same direction.

hammering

Place the metal or wire component on the bench block. Use the flat side of the ball-peen hammer to flatten the metal or wire. Use the ball head of a ball-peen hammer or texture hammer to create texture on the piece. Use a plastic or rawhide mallet to work-harden or flatten a piece without changing the surface.

metal stamping

Place the metal blank on the bench block. Hold the metal stamp perpendicular to the bench block with the image against the metal. Use a 2-pound brass hammer to strike the top of the stamp. For best results, stamp the image in a single blow.

oxidizing

Working in a well-ventilated area, follow the package directions for the specific patina solution you choose. Most require adding the solution to hot water and immersing the metal object for however long needed to obtain the shade you desire. You can also use the hard-boiled egg method described on page 14 ("From Plain to Pretty").

polishing

After oxidizing, polish your item with either a soft polishing cloth or fine steel wool (#0000) to bring out the shiny highlights on the metal.

tumbling

If you're planning on creating your own findings such as clasps and ear wires, you'll want to place them in a rotary tumbler to work-harden. Place the items in your tumbler with mixed stainless-steel shot, warm water, and a small amount of dishwashing liquid. Follow the directions for your tumbler on how much mixed stainless-steel shot and water to add. Always spread the mixed stainless-steel shot out on a dishtowel to dry before storing.

HOLE PUNCHING

using leather hole-punch pliers

Select the size of hole on the leather hole-punch tool if using a multihole version. Place the leather in the jaws of the pliers and squeeze.

using metal hole-punch pliers

If using metal hole-punch pliers, place the flat metal item between the jaws and squeeze. Sometimes it's helpful to insert a piece of thin plastic between your metal item and the pliers to prevent any accidental scratching of the metal. If using a screw-down hole punch, place the tool on a level surface. Insert the metal in between the open space of the hole punch and spin the handle slowly to lower the punch until it goes all the way through the metal. Spin the handle in the reverse direction to release your punched item.

hole punching (paper)

Insert the paper into the hole-punch pliers and squeeze the handles to create a hole.

SEWING

running stitch

To work a running stitch, pull the needle up from the bottom to the top of the fabric. Bring the needle down through the top of the fabric about ⅛–¼" (3.2–6.4mm) from where you started. Repeat as many times as needed to create a line of stitches.

whipstitch

Use a threaded needle to join the edges of two items. Bring the needle up from the bottom of the fabric through the top at a slight angle. Repeat the stitch about ⅛" (3.2 mm) or less from the previous stitch until the edges of the fabric are joined.

WIREWORK

using cones

String the ends of the strands of a multistrand necklace onto the loop of an eye pin or wrapped-loop wire. String 1 cone on the eye pin or wire. Form a wrapped loop at the other end of the cone that attaches to a jump ring or directly to one half of the clasp.

making a simple loop

Use the round-nose pliers to make a 90° bend in the wire about ¼" (6.4 cm) from the end. Grab the end of the wire with the pliers and roll the wire until the tip meets the bend.

making a double simple loop

Create a simple loop, but bend the wire about ½" (1.3 cm) from the end and, instead of ending the loop at the bend, continue around to make a second loop.

making a wrapped loop

Use your round-nose pliers to make a 90° bend in the wire about 1" (2.5 cm) from the end. Bend the wire as if you were creating a simple loop with a long tail. Place the loop flat in the jaws of chain- or flat-nose pliers and with your fingers, or another pair of pliers, wrap the tail around the wire below the loop 2 or 3 times. Trim.

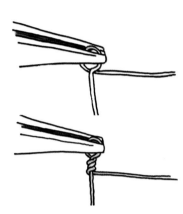

making a double-wrapped loop

Create a wrapped loop, but instead of trimming the wire, wind the wire back up over the previous wire wraps. Trim the tail below the loop.

making a briolette-wrapped loop

Center the top-drilled bead on 2" (5.1 cm) of wire. Bend both ends up forming a triangle over the bead. Wrap one wire around the other as if you were creating a wire-wrapped loop, trim the tail and pinch in the end with chain-nose pliers. Use the other wire to create a simple or wrapped loop. If creating a wrapped

loop, wrap the excess wire over the previous wire wraps, trim the wire, and pinch in the end.

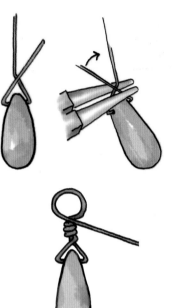

making a double-loop briolette-wrapped loop

Create a briolette-wrapped loop, using both wires to form the loop and the wrap.

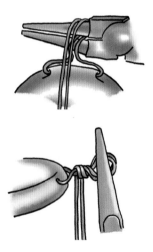

making a wrapped-loop dangle and link

To create a dangle, use 1 head pin or eye pin to string 1 or more beads; form a simple or wrapped loop. To create a link, connect the loop to the other component before closing the simple loop or completing the wrap of the wrapped loop.

making a spiral

Use the tip of your round-nose pliers to create a tiny loop. Hold the loop flat with your chain-nose pliers and coil the wire around the previous loop to create a spiral shape.

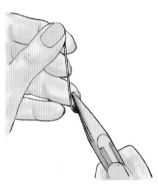

making a coil

Wrap the wire in tight, neat coils around a metal dowel or bail-making pliers, making sure each coil sits right next to the previous coil. Remove the coil and, if desired, flush cut the coil into shorter lengths or individual jump rings.

making a chain maille rosette

Connect 2 jump rings. Place them on top of one another. Open a third jump ring, string the 2 previous rings, and close the jump ring.

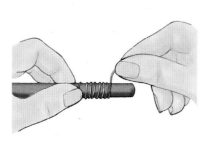

opening and closing a jump ring

Use 2 pairs of chain- or flat-nose pliers to gently twist the jump ring apart. Twist one end away from the other in opposite directions. Do not pull the ring apart as this will distort the ring shape.

wire wrapping

Use wire to secure the ends of beading cord, attach 2 metal pieces together, or to add embellishment. Bring the wire over and around the item being covered. If desired, add beads in between each rotation. Tuck in the ends of the wire.

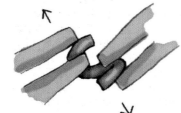

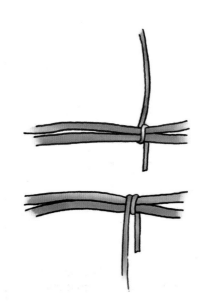

Meet the Designers

Michelle Mach loves creating whimsical jewelry with a mix of textures, shapes, and colors. The founding editor of the popular online community *Beading Daily*, she now works as a freelance editor, mainly for beading and jewelry books and magazines. More than 100 of her original designs have appeared in numerous magazines, including *Jewelry Stringing*, *BeadStyle*, *Beadwork*, *Bead-It Today*, and many others. She sells her jewelry online and in galleries and shops.
michellemach.com

Lorelei Eurto is a self-taught jewelry designer who views each piece of her jewelry as a collaboration with the artisans who make the components. She enjoys creating asymmetrical designs with focal points strategically placed to draw the eye. She coauthored *Bohemian-Inspired Jewelry* (Interweave, 2012). Her designs have also appeared in the books *Chain Style* (Interweave, 2009) and *Wire Style 2* (Interweave, 2011) and numerous magazines, including *BeadStyle, Jewelry Stringing, and Step by Step Beads*.
loreleieurtojewelry.com

Erin Siegel is a jewelry designer, author, and teacher living in Salem, Massachusetts, with her husband and daughter. She loves to create fun, fashion-forward jewelry for everyday wear. Erin coauthored the book *Bohemian-Inspired Jewelry* (Interweave, 2012). Her jewelry designs have been widely published in magazines, including *Jewelry Stringing* and *Belle Armoire Jewelry*. Erin designs jewelry projects for Ornamentea.com. Erin teaches at national events and retreats such as Bead Fest, artBLISS, and Bead Cruise.
erinsiegel.com

Jamie Hogsett is a designer and beading educator who creates for Antelope Beads. She is the former editor of *Jewelry Stringing* magazine, author of *Stringing Style* (Interweave, 2005), and coauthor of the Create Jewelry series (Interweave, 2007–2009), and *Show Your Colors* (Kalmbach, 2012). Jamie lives in Fort Collins, Colorado.
jlhogsett@yahoo.com

Denise Yezbak Moore is a self-taught artisan who incorporates romantic, sophisticated, and whimsical overtones into her pieces. Her designs have appeared in a wide variety of publications, including *Bead-It Today, Jewelry Stringing, Best of Stringing, Bead Star, Bead Unique, BeadStyle, Australian Beading Magazine, Jewelry Affaire*, and *Belle Armoire Jewelry*.
deniseyezbakmoore.blogspot.com

Erin Prais-Hintz loves to create something from nothing and believes that inspiration is everywhere. She has been featured in dozens of publications, including *Jewelry Stringing, Bead Trends, Bead-It Today, Bead Soup* (Kalmbach, 2012), *30 Minute Bracelets* (Lark, 2012), and *Showcase 500 Art Jewelry Necklaces* (Lark, 2013). She exhibits her work at Gallery Q in Stevens Point, Wisconsin, which she calls home with her husband and two kids.
tesoritrovati.com

Andrew Thornton is a professional fine artist who left New York City for rural Pennsylvania. His work can be seen in private collections around the globe. Andrew is the creative director and co-owner of Allegory Gallery, part bead store and part art gallery, in Ligonier, Pennsylvania.
andrew-thornton.blogspot.com

Molly Schaller has been beading ever since she was an elementary school student and loves watching a project come together. She lives in Indiana with her three creative kids, firefighter husband, feisty terrier, and fuzzy lop-eared rabbit.
craftinglife.blogspot.com

Erin Strother is a graphic designer living happily in Southern California with her supportive husband, George, and their disobedient dog, Swiffer. She loves working with a wide variety of materials and experimenting with unique designs.
studioEgallery.etsy.com

Barb Switzer has been learning, teaching, and practicing beadwork since 1995. She works as a jewelry designer, columnist, graphic designer, and illustrator. She was a freelance editor for *Wirework* and *Simply Beads* magazines, for the books *Earrings, Earrings, Earrings!* (Annie's, 2009) and *Four Seasons of Beading* (Annie's, 2009), and as the technical editor for an upcoming Lark Masters Series book about wire. Barb works from her home in rural Northern California.
beadswitzer@gmail.com

Cindy Wimmer is a designer with a passion for combining vintage elements with modern wire design. Her jewelry has been published internationally, and she has contributed designs to the books *Wire Style 2* (Interweave, 2011) and *Bead Soup* (Kalmbach, 2012). She is the cofounder of artBLISS, hosting workshops in the Washington, D.C, area. Cindy is author of *The Missing Link* (Interweave, 2013) and the 2014 Featured Artist for *Step by Step Wire Jewelry* magazine. She lives in Virginia with her husband and four sons.
cindywimmer.com

Resources

The list below gives the resources for the materials used in the projects. In a few cases where the exact materials are no longer available, we've suggested similar materials that will work. Be sure to ask the shops if you don't find the item you need. They may have additional inventory not posted online or be able to suggest an alternative product.

This list includes a few wholesale shops; these may require a sales license and a minimum purchase amount. Most offer lists of brick-and-mortar and online retail shops that stock their items as well. Your own local bead shop is a valuable resource.

Vintage materials provide special shopping challenges. While you may not find the exact item, you can find similar materials on eBay and Etsy and at antique malls, flea markets, and garage sales.

FINDINGS

Bail and penny earrings (page 5)
Bails: Metal Me This. Penny chain: Ornamentea. Post ear wires: Fusionbeads.com. Faceted copper fire-polished rounds: Rings & Things.

Bead cap (acorn) necklace (page 6)
Bead caps: B'Sue Boutiques. Leaf: C-Koop Beads. Vintage chain: AD Adornments. Ceramic rounds: Michaels.

Cone pendant (page 6)
Kazuri ceramic round: Antelope Beads. Chain: Vintaj Natural Brass Co. Cone: Fusionbeads.com.

Knot-cup earrings (page 9)
Ring bands: Rings & Things. Knot cups: Fire Mountain Gems and Beads. Mookaite: Lima Beads. Ear wires: Vintaj Natural Brass Co.

Spacer bar earrings (page 13)
Swarovski jet crystal rounds: Fusionbeads.com. Silver crystal rondelles: Lima Beads. Ear wires: Bead Cache. Spacer bars: Rings & Things.

FROM PLAIN TO PRETTY (PAGE 14)

Silver filigree: Rings & Things. Copper-plated wire flowers: Primitive Earth Beads. Turquoise howlite rounds: Michaels. Washers: Harbor Freight. Brass flowers: Vintaj Natural Brass Co. Spacer bars: Michaels. Patina and Gilder's Paste: B'Sue Boutiques. Brass jump ring: Michaels. Leather: The Lipstick Ranch.

NO HOLE? NO PROBLEM (PAGE 17)

Filigree: Vintaj Natural Brass Co. Bezel tape: Artbeads.com. Bezel: B'Sue Boutiques. Similar cabochons: Fire Mountain Gems and Beads.

DIY CHAIN (PAGE 19)

Bail chain
Bails: Fire Mountain Gems and Beads.

Bracelet spacer-bar chain
Spacer bars: Rings & Things. Marquis connectors: MK Beads.

Charm (safety pin) chain
Charms: B'Sue Boutiques. Foldover chain connectors: Fancy Gems and Findings.

Eye-pin chain
Green glass beads: Raven's Journey International.

THE PROJECTS

Amy Ayres (page 88)
All brass components: Vintaj Natural Brass Co. Sari silk: Brea Bead Works. Superglue and shell by Halcraft USA (Michaels).

Variation: Pewter owl: Green Girl Studios. Ribbon and flower pendant: Jess Imports. Similar chain: Ornamentea. Brass components: Vintaj Natural Brass Co. Lucite flower: Vintage Meadow Artworks (Lima Beads).

Ancient Artifacts (page 84)
Blanks, brass discs, jump rings: Ring & Things. Similar clasp: Artbeads.com. Ceramic, jasper, spacers, similar crystal, similar ear wires, eye pins: Fire Mountain Gems and Beads.

Variation: Guitar pick blanks: Rings & Things.

Botanica (page 52)
Lampwork tube: Magdalena Ruiz. Glass head pins: Gardanne Beads. Filigree bead caps: Vintaj Natural Brass Co. Clasp and copper coins: Michaels. Seed beads: Fusionbeads.com. Tin bead: Glass Garden Beads. Flower bead cap: C-Koop Beads. Lampwork spacer: Kelley's Bead Studio. Similar green glass briolettes: Maya Honey. Flexible beading wire: Soft Flex Company. Crimp tubes: Beadalon.

Variation: All materials: Ornamentea.

Branching Out *(page 90)*
Pendant: Humblebeads. Bird, jade, chain, flexible beading wire, clasp, crimp tubes and covers: Fusionbeads.com. Spacer bar: Artbeads.com. Aventurine: Rings & Things. Quartz and Swarovski crystal: Accents Beads. Head pins, jump rings, and wire: Monsterslayer.

Brazen Blooms *(page 68)*
All brass components: Vintaj Natural Brass Co. Sari silk: Brea Bead Works. Beads by Halcraft USA (Michaels).

California Poppy *(page 24)*
Flower: Lisa Kan. Frames: Vintaj Natural Brass Co. Chain: Lima Beads. Clasp: Fusionbeads.com. Leaves: Raven's Journey International. Orange rounds: Michaels. Filigree: Ornamentea. Ribbon, thread, embroidery floss, interfacing: Jo-Ann Fabric and Craft. Swarovski crystal bicones: Fusionbeads.com. Silver round: Fire Mountain Gems and Beads.

Central Spark *(page 38)*
Bead frames: Fire Mountain Gems and Beads. Crystal rondelle beads: Artbeads.com. Brass beads: Hands of the Hills. Gauged wire: Monsterslayer. Crimp tubes and flexible beading wire: Michaels. Similar clasp and jump rings: Unkamen Supplies.

Variation: Shells: Michaels. Crystals and ear wires: Fusionbeads.com.

Cognificent *(page 92)*
Cuff, gunmetal and antiqued copper gears by Idea-ology. Copper-plated rounds and daisy spacers: Hobby Lobby. Propeller: B'Sue Boutiques. Brass and copper gears, copper glass beads: Rings & Things. Gunmetal bead cap, brass hive bead cap: Ornamentea. Hexagon spacers: Bead Cache. Dark brass gear, brass saucer, brass flower spacer: Vintaj Natural Brass Co. Head pins: Fire Mountain Gems and Beads. Etched bead caps: Metal Me This.

Variation: Cuff, brass splats, bead caps: Ornamentea. Flowers: B'Sue Boutiques. Bead caps: Ornamentea. Glass: Raven's Journey International. Amethyst: Lima Beads. Spacers: Hobby Lobby.

Connect the Dots *(page 80)*
Red rounds, turquoise ovals by Halcraft USA (Michaels). Eye pins and bead caps: TierraCast. Chain and jump rings: Vintaj Natural Brass Co. Ceramic rounds: Golem Design Studio.

Constellation *(page 106)*
Swarovski crystal pearls, head pins, eye pins, jump rings: Fusionbeads.com. Clasp: The Ring Lord (theringlord.com).

Dalle de Verre *(page 94)*
Clasp: C-Koop Beads. Ball-chain clasps: Nina Designs. Seed beads: Beyond Beadery. Ceramic round by Elaine Ray: Ornamentea. Faceted Montana blue glass: Raven's Journey International. Blue goldstone: Fire Mountain Gems and Beads. Pearls, crimp covers, spacer bars: Fusionbeads.com. Copper faceted rounds: Rings & Things. Daisy spacers and shell rounds: Hobby Lobby. Chain: Primitive Earth Beads.

Dancing Damselfly *(page 40)*
Brass components: Vintaj Natural Brass Co. Linen thread: Royalwood, Ltd. Flower ceramic bead: Golem Design Studio. Pendant and all other ceramic beads: Gaea Beads.

Downtown Arts District *(page 116)*
Lampwork: Shirley Glass Beads. Crimp tube, crimp covers, and flexible beading wire: Artbeads.com. Hill tribe silver: Fusionbeads.com. Sterling jump rings: Atlantis Glass and Bead. Bead caps: Glamour Puss Beads. Sterling wire: Monsterslayer. Similar S-clasp and jump rings: Unkamen Supplies.

Enchanted Forest *(page 74)*
Seed beads: Beyond Beadery. Peanut beads: Whimbeads.com. lampwork-glass beads: Patti Cahill. Crystal pearls: Fusionbeads.com. Polymer clay rondelles: Humblebeads. Polymer clay rounds: Pam Wynn. Flexible beading wire: Soft Flex Company. Cord ends, head pins, and crimp covers: Antelope Beads.

Fiesta *(page 122)*
All materials: Ornamentea.

Fringe Benefits *(page 44)*
Chain, jump rings, crimp tubes: Rings & Things. Beadalon wire, coins, and coral by Halcraft USA (Michaels). Box clasps: A Grain of Sand.

Variation: Chain, box clasp: Fire Mountain Gems and Beads. Flowers: Raven's Journey International. Glass leaves: Fusionbeads.com.

Gypsy Girl *(page 50)*
Gunmetal rounds and snap clasps: Bead Cache. Gunmetal head pins: Rings & Things. Agate: Dakota Stones. Teal glass: Raven's Journey International. Sequins: Michelle Mach. Gunmetal chain: Artbeads.com. Rondelles: Fusionbeads.com.

Hanawa *(page 46)*
Suede lace: Michaels. Chain: AD Adornments. Ribbon ends: Ornamentea. Similar crepe cord: Fabric Tales. Clasp: Ruby Mountain Metal. Jump rings and cord ends: Vintaj Natural Brass Co.

I Dream of the Sea *(page 112)*
Polymer clay connector and head pins: Humblebeads. Clasp: Green Girl Studios. Seed beads: Whimbeads. Beadalon wire, star head pins: Beadalon. Crimp tubes, jump rings, spacers, coral beads, similar mother-of-pearl discs, similar shell beads: Rings & Things. Glass beads: Nirvana Beads.

Key West (page 104)
Brass components: Vintaj Natural Brass Co. Wood beads: Beads and Pieces. Porcelain discs: Elaine Ray (Ornamentea). Clasps: Rings & Things. Small copper rounds and daisy spacers: Hobby Lobby. Large copper rounds: Miss Fickle Media. Seed beads: Beyond Beadery.

Variation: Chain: Chain Gallery.

Leaves of Gold (page 48)
Seed beads: Bead Biz. Wood rounds: City Beads. Linen cord and bails: Ornamentea. Sodalite: Fire Mountain Gems and Beads. Button: Jo-Ann Fabric and Craft.

Lotus Blossom (page 30)
Chain and bead: Fusionbeads.com. Clasp: Fire Mountain Gems and Beads. Lotus flower: Kabela Design. Cord: Ornamentea. Bezel: B'Sue Boutiques. Earring hoop: The Beadin' Path. Blank: Vintaj Natural Brass Co. Jump rings, spacers, and head pin: Bead Cache. Buttons: Jo-Ann Fabric and Craft.

Mademoiselle Fleur (page 118)
Swarovski crystal pearls and clasp: Artbeads.com. Filigree: Kabela Design. Bead caps: B'Sue Boutiques. Jump rings, eye pins, and head pin: Vintaj Natural Brass Co. Copper round: Hobby Lobby.

Variation: Ceramic round: Golem Design Studio. Bead caps and leaf: B'Sue Boutiques. Gear: Rings & Things. Chain: Vintaj Natural Brass Co. Green glass beads: Raven's Journey International. Green disc: Artbeads.com. Bead cap: The Potomac Bead Co.

Maya (page 96)
All materials: Ornamentea.

May Flowers (page 42)
Swarovski crystals and pearls: Fusionbeads.com. Jump rings, head pins, and ear wires: Vintaj Natural Brass Co. Ring bands: B'Sue Boutiques. Flowers: The Beadin' Path.

Variation: Glass leaves: Fusionbeads.com. Copper rounds: Hobby Lobby.

Meditation Garden (page 54)
Polymer clay rondelles: Humblebeads. Brass links, rings, bars and chain: Vintaj Natural Brass Co. Aluminum discs: Lillypilly Designs. Flower-end head pin: Shiana. Ball-end head pins: Saki Silver. Super New Glue: Antelope Beads.

Variation: Same resources as main project.

Metal Mixology (page 114)
Cones, chain: Nunn Design. Clasp: Fusionbeads.com. Rounds: Hobby Lobby. Eye pins and brass jump ring: Vintaj Natural Brass Co. Wildfire beading thread: Michaels.

Midnight Waltz (page 64)
Bead caps: B'Sue Boutiques. Chain: Ornamentea. Glass: Bead Cache. Ear wires, eye pins, brass chain: Vintaj Natural Brass Co. Copper rounds: Fusionbeads.com. Ear wires: Nunn Design.

Variation: Copper bead caps: Ornamentea. Pewter spacers: Lima Beads. Swarovski crystal pearls: Fusionbeads.com.

Off the Cuff (page 108)
Raku beads: XAZ Bead Co. Crystals: Fire Mountain Gems and Beads. Leather cuff, copper head pins, ring blanks by Halcraft USA (Michaels).

Variation: Leather cuff: Michaels. Head pins: Fire Mountain Gems and Beads. Glass: Lima Beads.

Owl at the Moon (page 126)
Pendant: Still Point Works. Ceramic bead: Antelope Beads. Head pins: Miss Fickle Media. Coins, bead frames, crimps: Michaels. Similar glass leaves: Artebella Surplus. Jade: Lima Beads. Toggle: Fusionbeads.com. Similar vintage chain: Shop Etsy or vintage/antique suppliers. Copper wire: Patina Queen. Flexible beading wire: Soft Flex Company.

A Passel of Tassels (page 100)
Cord: Jewelry Accord. Lampwork discs: Indian Creek Glass. Jump rings and ear wires: Vintaj Natural Brass Co.

Variation: Ceramic beads by Jean Christen: Bellingham Bead Bazaar. Glass rounds: Five Sisters.

Poet Laureate (page 86)
Cord, cord ends, pearls, wire: Fusionbeads.com. Filigree, leaf connector, jump rings, chain link, flowers: Vintaj Natural Brass Co. Painted disc: Michelle Mach. Clasp: Ornamentea. Brass head pins: Fire Mountain Gems and Beads.

Queen of Thorns (page 110)
Beads and clasp: Allegory Gallery. Swarovski crystal pendant, jump rings, crimps: Fusionbeads.com. Cones: Cherry Tree Beads.

Retro Mix (page 32)
Seed beads: Beyond Beadery. Glass rounds, crystal pearls, Lucite rounds, crimp covers, and flexible beading wire: Fusionbeads.com. Lampwork beads: Lori Greenberg. Gold-plated pewter beads, chain, gauged wire, and eye pins: Antelope Beads. Toggle clasp: Springall Adventures. Slide-tube clasps: Bead Cache.

Rings Around the Monarch (page 66)
Lampwork focal: Kerri Fuhr Beads. Carnelian: Beads Direct Online. Beadalon wire and seed beads: Michaels. Crimp tubes and covers: Rings & Things. Aluminum jump rings: Unkamen Supplies. Brass jump rings and clasps: Vintaj Natural Brass Co. Similar silk cord: Ornamentea. Copper jump rings: Lima Beads.

Sadie's Secret (page 102)
Swarovski rhinestone rounds and all other materials: Ornamentea.

Searching for Simplicity (page 124)
Beads, head pins, and seed beads: Allegory Gallery. Crimp covers and crimps: Fusionbeads.com. Cones, clasp, bails: Cherry Tree Beads. Pendant: Swoondimples.

Secrets of Jade *(page 72)*
All materials, including similar filigree: Fusionbeads.com.

Variation: Swarovski crystal and pearls: Swarovski North America. Chandeliers: Michaels. Polymer clay rondelles: Humblebeads. Clasp and jump rings: Fire Mountain Gems and Beads. Flexible beading wire and crimp tubes: Beadalon.

Silver Lining *(page 120)*
Porcelain bead cap: Chinook Jewelry. Enamel bead cap: Gardanne Beads. Copper bead cap by Patricia Healey (Lima Beads). Blue teardrops, clear teardrops, chain, clasp: Clouds: Kabo Design. Copper seed beads: Beyond Beadery.

Variation: Silver filigree bead cap: Hobby Lobby. Red bead cap: C-Koop Beads.

Sweet Soirée *(page 26)*
Ceramic beads by Keith O'Connor: The Beadin' Path. Cones and toggle: Nina Designs. Swarovski crystals: Fusionbeads.com. Turquoise, Artistic Wire craft wire, head pins: Michaels. Spacers: Hand of the Hills. Flexible beading wire: Soft Flex Company. Crimps: Beadalon.

Variation: Rondelles: Humblebeads. Brass beads and head pins: Vintaj Natural Brass Co. Clasp: Green Girl Studio. Flowers, seed beads, flexible beading wire: Fusionbeads.com. Spacers: Springall Adventures. Enameled rounds: C-Koop Beads. Lampwork rondelles: Lori Greenberg. Lucite flowers: Bead Cache.

Tidal Treasures *(page 57)*
Flexible beading wire, crimp tubes: Beadalon. Clasp: Handfast. Similar teardrops: Beadaholique. Seed beads, gauged wire, pearls: Fusionbeads.com. Peanut beads: Whimbeads. Silver beads: Shiana. Cone: Nina Designs. Fish bead and coral link: Green Girl Studios.

Variation: Glass: Raven's Journey International. Clasp: Artbeads.com. Chain: Rings & Things. Spacers: Hobby Lobby. Copper petal and brass filigree bead caps: Ornamentea. Copper filigree bead caps: B'Sue Boutiques. Copper etched bead caps: Lima Beads. Metal seed beads: Beyond Beadery. Wood beads: Beads and Pieces. Tigereye: Fire Mountain Gems and Beads.

Tuesday Night Book Club *(page 78)*
Enameled leather cord end: C-Koop Beads. Filigree diamond, charms, brass jump rings: Vintaj Natural Brass Co. Cords, cord end clasp, copper jump rings: Lima Beads. Paper: Hobby Lobby. Wire: Artbeads.com. Filigree tube: B'Sue Boutiques.

Two to Tango *(page 36)*
Eye pins, jump rings, ear wires: Vintaj Natural Brass Co. Spacers: Hobby Lobby. Glass: Raven's Journey International. Similar ceramic disc (donut): Fire Mountain Gems and Beads.

Variation: Wood tubes: Michaels. Brass connectors: Kabela Designs.

Vertebracelet *(page 82)*
All materials: Fusionbeads.com.

Vintage Revival *(page 128)*
Similar-style vintage brooch: Shop antiques stores, Etsy, or other vintage suppliers. Pin converters: GS Boutique. Pearls and crystal: Fusionbeads.com. Rhinestone rondelles: Artbeads.com. Clasp: AD Adornments. Chain: Star's Beads. Crimp tubes and flexible beading wire: Michaels. Gauged wire: Monsterslayer. Similar S-clasp and jump rings: Unkamen Supplies.

Washer Woman *(page 62)*
Copper washers: Harbor Freight. Stainless steel and bronze washers, stainless ball chain and connector, jump rings, toggle bar: The Ring Lord. Iolite, pearl, wire, head pin: Fire Mountain Gems and Beads.

Vintage key: Ashbury Lane. Copper ball chain and connector, quartz: Rings & Things. Brass cable chain: Brassologie.

Westward Bound *(page 28)*
All materials: Ornamentea.

Variation (earrings): All materials: Ornamentea.

Variation (necklace): Wood: Beads and Pieces. Clasp: Fusionbeads.com. Amethyst: JM Imports. Ribbon and cord ends: Ornamentea. Jump rings, head pins, wire: Vintaj Natural Brass Co. Leather: Hobby Lobby.

Wishing Tree *(page 60)*
Porcelain pendant: Marsha Neal Studio. Amethyst and tree pendant by Ezel Findings: Lima Beads. Bird: The Lipstick Ranch. Bead cap: Hobby Lobby. Clasps: Rings & Things. Apatite: Happy Mango Beads. Ceramic by Elaine Ray: Ornamentea. Small blue beads, Montana blue, big purple: Raven's Journey International.

Variation: Ear wires: Lima Beads. Birds: The Lipstick Ranch. Flowers, jump rings, wire, head pins: Vintaj Natural Brass Co.

Wish Me Luck *(page 98)*
Bezel by SLK Art Mechanique: ICE Resin. Heart pendant: Diane Hawkey. Gemstones: Beads Direct Online. Flexible beading wire: Soft Flex Company. Crimp tubes, green pearls: Rings & Things. Similar rolo chain: Beadaholique. TierraCast daisy spacers, hook: Goody Beads. Jump rings: Vintaj Natural Brass Co.

Zero Hour *(page 70)*
Leather, wire: Rings & Things. Copper washers: Harbor Freight. Jump rings: The Ring Lord. Copper rounds: Fusionbeads.com. Similar toggle bar: Miss Fickle Media.

Start Shopping

If you don't see what you need online, be sure to ask the shop. Not all shops list their entire inventory online.

Accents Beads
accentsbeads.com

AD Adornments
adadornments.com

Allegory Gallery
allegorygallery.com

Antelope Beads
antelopebeads.com

Artbeads.com
artbeads.com

Artebella Surplus
artebellasurplus.etsy.com

Ashbury Lane
ashburylane.etsy.com

Atlantis Glass and Bead
atlantisglassandbead.etsy
.com

Beadaholique
beadaholique.com

Beadalon
beadalon.com

Bead Biz
beadbiz.org

Bead Cache
bead-cache.com

The Beadin' Path
beadinpath.com

Beads and Pieces
beadsandpieces.com

Beads Direct Online
beadsdirectonline.com

Bellingham Bead Bazaar
bellinghambeadbazaar
.com

Beyond Beadery
beyondbeadery.com

Bokamo Designs
bokamodesigns.com

Brassologie
brassologie.com

Brea Bead Works
breabeadworks.com

Bronwen Heilman
bronwenheilman.com

B'Sue Boutiques
bsueboutiques.com

Chain Gallery
chaingallery.com

Cherry Tree Beads
cherrytreebeads.com

Chinook Jewelry
chinookjewelry.com

City Beads
citybeadsny.com

C-Koop Beads
ckoopbeads.com

Dakota Stones
dakotastones.com

Diane Hawkey
dianehawkey.etsy.com

Fabric Tales
fabrictales.com

Fancy Gems and Findings
gemsandfindings.com

Fire Mountain Gems and Beads
firemountaingems.com

Five Sisters
fivesisters.etsy.com

Fusionbeads.com
fusionbeads.com

Gaea Beads
gaea.cc

Gardanne Beads
GardanneBeads.etsy.com

Glamour Puss Beads
glamourpussbeads.etsy
.com

Glass Garden Beads
glassgardenbeads.com

Golem Design Studio
golemstudio.com

Goody Beads
goodybeads.com

A Grain of Sand
agrainofsand.com

Green Girl Studios
greengirlstudios.com

GS Boutique
gsboutique.etsy.com

Halcraft USA
halcraft.com

Handfast
handfast.biz

Hand of the Hills
hohbead.com

Happy Mango Beads
happymangobeads.com

Harbor Freight
harborfreight.com

Hobby Lobby
hobbylobby.com

Home Depot
homedepot.com

Humblebeads
humblebeads.com

ICE Resin
iceresin.com

Indian Creek Glass
outwest.etsy.com

JM Imports
jmimports.com

Jess Imports
jessimports.com

Jewelry Accord
jewelryaccord.etsy.com

Jo-Ann Fabric and Craft
joann.com

Kabela Design
kabeladesign.com

Kelley's Bead Studio
kelleysbeads.etsy.com

Kerri Fuhr Beads
kerrifuhr.com

Lillypilly Designs
lillypillydesigns.com

Lima Beads
limabeads.com

The Lipstick Ranch
thelipstickranch.com

Lisa Kan Designs
lisakan.com

Lori Greenberg
www.lorigreenberg.com

Magdalena Ruiz
magdalenaruiz.etsy.com

Marsha Neal Studio
marshanealstudio.com

Maya Honey
mayahoney.etsy.com

Metal Me This
metalmethis.etsy.com

Michaels
michaels.com

Michelle Mach Jewelry
& Gifts
michellemach.com

Miss Fickle Media
missficklemedia.etsy.com

Mixed Metal Blanks
mixedmetalblankscom
.etsy.com

MKBeads
mkbeads.com

Monsterslayer
monsterslayer.com

Nina Designs
ninadesigns.com

Nirvana Beads
nirvanabeads.com

Nunn Design
(wholesale only)
nunndesign.com

Ornamentea
ornamentea.com

Pam Wynn
pamwynn.etsy.com

Patina Queen
patinaqueen.com

Patti Cahill
patticahill.etsy.com

The Potomac Bead
Company
potomacbeads.com

Primitive Earth Beads
primativeearthbeads.com

Raven's Journey
International
theravenstore.com

The Ring Lord
theringlord.com

Rings & Things
rings-things.com

Rio Grande
riogrande.com

Royalwood, LTD
royalwoodltd.com

Ruby Mountain Metal
rubymountainmetal.etsy
.com

Saki Silver
sakisilver.com

Shiana
shiana.com

Shirley Glass Beads
shirleyglassbeads.etsy.com

Soft Flex Company
softflexco.com

Sonoran Beads
sonoranbeads.com

Springall Adventures
(505) 757-6520

Star's Beads
starsbeads.com

Still Point Works
stillpointworks.etsy.com

Swarovski North
America
create-your-style.com

Swoondimples
(Heather Wynn)
heatherwynn.com

TierraCast
(wholesale only)
tierracast.com

Unkamen Supplies
unkamensupplies.etsy.com

Via Murano
viamurano.com

Vintaj Natural Brass Co.
(wholesale only)
vintaj.com

Whimbeads
whimbeads.com

XAZ Bead Co.
xazbead.com

ZnetShows
znetshows.com

Index

design custom handmade jewelry
with these hot titles from Interweave

**THE ART OF
FORGOTTEN THINGS**
Creating Jewelry from Objects
with a Past
Melanie Doerman
ISBN 978-1-59668-548-2, $24.95

RESIN ALCHEMY
Innovative Techniques for Mixed-
Media and Jewelry Artists
Susan Lenart Kazmer
ISBN 978-1-59668-644-1, $24.95

BOHEMIAN-INSPIRED JEWELRY
50 Designs Using Leather,
Ribbon, and Cords
Lorelei Eurto and Erin Siegel
ISBN 978-1-59668-498-0, $22.99

LAPIDARY JOURNAL
**JEWELRY
ARTIST**

Check out *Jewelry Artist*, a trusted guide
to the art of gems, jewelry making, design,
beads, minerals, and more. Whether you
are a beginner, an experienced artisan,
or in the jewelry business, *Jewelry
Artist* can take you to a whole new level.
JEWELRYARTISTMAGAZINE.COM

 **Jewelry** Making Daily

Jewelry Making Daily is the ultimate online community for anyone interested
in creating handmade jewelry. Get tips from industry experts, download free
step-by-step projects, check out video demos, discover sources for supplies,
and more! Sign up at **JEWELRYMAKINGDAILY.COM**.